THE

PRIVILEGED

PREDATOR

-by Lorin Preston Gill

THE PRIVILEGED PREDATOR

This book is self published. It never got rejected by Random House, Penguin or any other traditional publishers. I have a problem with rejection. I wasn't about to remortgage my house to get it published by a vanity publisher.

You might notice a few "omissions" - things like page numbers. Sorry. The next time you're waiting in the doctor's office, grab a pen from the receptionist and write the page numbers in yourself if you need to. Return the pen.

Reviews from other authors are not evident but if you want some praises, here you go:

My dentist Paul thought the book was "pretty good".

My daughter Katie thought it was "OK".

Ed Masi smiled as he read it.

PREFACE

The title Superthief that has been used to describe Jack MacLean, was created by Florida law enforcement officials before he was caught.

The sheer number of burglaries perpetrated and their methodical planning led to southern Florida law enforcement's labeling Jack MacLean as a Superthief. How Jack circumvented the weight, heat, and motion detection sensors in the Wold family's home security system still confounds police and helped reinforce MacLean's Superthief title.

Josh Fox's 9/10/2011 list of the "Top 10 Infamous Cat Burglars" in America, awarded Jack the number one ranking. According to Fox, "Jack MacLean was the most prolific burglar in United States history".

Jack has never apologized to any of his victims for breaking into their homes, stealing their valuables, and disrupting their lives.

Estimates of the valuables stolen from Florida homes range from $125,000,000.00 to $133,000,000.00. Jack robbed as many as 2,000 residences before being caught. He was more than a casual thief. Superthief, however, does not mean that MacLean's was a Superhero. Jack got caught*.

When did Jack transition from the Kick-the-car game to robbing the Wold residence? When did Jack start invading people's homes and become a professional thief? What drove him to commit felony crimes that are punishable by life in prison?

*In 1979 MacLean was "convicted by plea" to felony burglary and felony robbery charges in Florida. He was sentenced to fifteen years that were served concurrently. He admitted guilt to a 1991 2nd degree felony burglary in Arizona from which he received another fifteen year sentence. Jack does not deny his burglaries. He is currently in jail in Broward County Florida facing two felony charges with the possibility of two life sentences.

Under our pictures in our Reading High School yearbook are listed our accomplishments and life's goals. As might be expected, many of us didn't enter the professions that we envisioned when we were eighteen.

Some achieved their early desires:

- Denise wanted to become a nurse and she became a nurse.

- Jeff was destined for a music career and became a college music teacher.

Some got close:

- Rick wanted to be a stock broker and entered real estate.

- Charlie wanted to be a business administrator and entered publishing.

Others took a different course than they anticipated:

- Cindy and Tyke hadn't decided what they wanted to do. They still haven't decided - why rush?

- Jack wanted to go to an aero-technical school but became a burglar.

READING

Reading Massachusetts is a town of

twenty-five thousand people (twenty thousand in 1965) located ten miles north of Boston. Incorporated June 10, 1644 Reading was named after the town of Reading England.

Like many New England towns Reading has a grand white church that is the focal point of the town's center. The Old South Methodist Church oversees the comings and goings of Reading's residents. The Methodist Church's three prominent steeple clocks can be observed from all the roads that feed traffic to the center of town. The bells of the old church sound on the hour and on Sunday to remind residents to attend services. The church was built in 1800.

Someone sitting in the common could listen for hours, days, or longer and not hear a car horn or car tires screech. One could wait forever and never hear a gun shot or a plea for help. Reading, you see, is a polite town.

The cozy brick, Georgian Revival style town hall and old library sit patiently across Woburn Street while the town's stores cater to unhurried shoppers.

A light, recently fallen snow made the

common as white as the church. The pure white covering seems to slow and quiets life in the town. Cold of winter keeps all of the townspeople from sitting on any of the nine benches that circle the common.

In the summer, the common's benches allow the townspeople to watch the cars pass by, while a large American flag flies atop a tall white flag pole. When the snow abdicates and the season warms in late spring, a few people will enjoy the bench's comfort as they rest or lunch outside, appreciating that winter has finally departed. Large oak and maple trees will temper the sun's rays for the common's few visitors.

In the summer the common's grass will be perfectly mowed. No trash will litter The Reading Common. If town employees do not remove stray litter from the common in time, residents will remove it on their own volition. Reading residents genuinely love their town and are proud of it.

In the fall after the maples do their beautiful New England dance, fallen leaves will be raked and removed. Winter will return all too soon.

No rallies or revolutions were ever initiated on the Reading common. Politicians are not allowed to display campaign signs. Reading is a peaceful town.

In 1965 most of Reading Municipal High School graduates continued their educations at institutions of higher learning. After leaving school in 1965 some of the graduates stayed in Reading and had families. Other graduates moved to nearby towns, some moved to Maine and New Hampshire, some to England and Sweden, some to California, Texas, and, yes, Florida.

Median family income in Reading in 2010 was $117,477, with less than 1% of the population living below US poverty level. Reading residents are well off financially with most living in comfortable single family homes. The only year Reading's population ever decreased was in 1861, when the US Civil War began.

Between 1961 and 1965 Reading High

School students were 99% White, less than 1% Asian, and less than 1% Black.

The Parker Tavern, built in 1694, survives as a museum.

Joshua Eaton was killed in the Battle of Saratoga in 1777 in the Revolutionary War. The Joshua Eaton Grammar School was named after him.

Four lane Route 28 furnished Reading residents with access to Boston. Later, eight lane Route 93 was built. Route 93 provided a faster route to "the city". Six lane Route 128 circles Reading. Route 128 provides access to the Massachusetts Technological Highway. In 1965, Route 128 businesses provided Reading families with high paying jobs in companies that were building "The New Machine".

In the 1960s and '70s many Reading fathers worked in Boston in banks, brokerage houses, insurance, finance and other professional businesses. In the 1950s, 60s, and 70s, men wore suits and ties to work in Boston, even on hot summer days. Women wore skirts and blouses or dresses that covered their knees. Cleavage was never exposed.

Fathers worked hard and most mothers stayed home to care for us Baby Boomers. Dad would count off the train stops on his homeward bound ride from Boston: Wyoming, Melrose, Melrose Highlands, Greenwood, Wakefield and finally, Reading. Fathers anticipated an enthusiastic welcome from their children, a warm kiss from mom, and a dry Martini before dinner.

Reading was a dry town until 1970 when it got its first liquor store (Massachusetts residents, for some reason, call them "package stores"). No liquor was sold in any restaurants or stores in Reading before 1970. The town has never had a barroom.

Until he bought Billy A.'s house on Haverhill Street, Boston Celtics basketball star Bill Russell lived in a small house on Main Street next to a gas station. Russell's house was not on the right side of the tracks. Reading homes, that are on the right side of the tracks, are stately two and three story Colonials with ten to fourteen rooms and stone foundations.

Even Billy A.'s house, though large and impressive, was not in Reading's finest area. The only other Black family in Reading owned a gas station and garage. Reading was not lily white but it was definitely White.

When I was thirteen years old my family moved from very rural Merrimack, New Hampshire to Reading. In Merrimack, we were poor. Merrimack was backward and unsophisticated. In Merrimack, my interests were limited to church, Boy Scouts, and the tiniest of libraries. The town's wealthiest family owned a saw mill and drove a Cadillac deVille. The town's largest employer was a chicken processing plant. Locals called it the "chicken pluckin' factory".

An old joke: "How do can you identify a wealthy Merrimack family? Wealthy Merrimack families have two junk cars in the driveway." Later Merrimack would become gentrified because of a Budweiser plant, Route 93, and it's proximity to good paying jobs in Massachusetts.

Reading, on the other hand, had excellent

schools, residents were professionals, single family homes were large and well cared for. The town library (founded in 1791) had three levels and a large magazine section. Ninety-eight precent of Reading students graduated from high school and most went on to college. There is a large downtown area with all sorts of stores. There was a community center and there was access to good health care. There were no junk cars in Reading driveways.

Reading unfortunately produced one of the country's most prolific thieves who burglarized homes with impunity. The serial burglar is Jack MacLean.

Jack and I graduated from Reading High School in 1965. He missed our fiftieth high school reunion because he was in prison, where he may be held for the rest of his life if he gets convicted of recent criminal charges. Jack lived in Reading from the time he was born until just after high school.

Jack MacLean was my friend and I knew him well.

PRETTY BABY

Jack Maclean was one of twenty Mellins Baby Food babies.

Most people have never heard of Mellins Baby Food since they ceased operation in 1927. Efforts to revive the company in 1945 failed. Gerber, Beech nut, and Mead Johnson (Pablum) proved too great a challenge for Mellins' revival. Gerber and Beech Nut were entrenched in post World War II America. Mellins' national campaign to find new babies gave the company some notoriety but their product fell short of the established competition and Mellins no longer had a national distribution chain. The Mellins resurrection failed.

Mellins, before 1927, distributed pictures of infants and toddlers as promotional items. Unlike the one Gerber Baby, Mellins' twenty images were used on their baby food containers, in advertising, and trading cards - people traded them like baseball cards. Parents compared their own children to the Mellins babies to see which Mellins baby their child most looked like.

Mellins had an open contest with a prize (unknown) for anyone who could identify the gender of all twenty babies. The odds were 2 to the twentieth power or 1 in 1,048,576 of guessing all twenty's sex. No one ever won. The difficulty of guessing the correct gender was exacerbated by the babies' clothes. All the babies wore white night gowns. Hair length was not a help either.

Ruth Gordon (Harold and Maud) and Humphrey Bogart were Mellins babies. Bogart's mother was an illustrator for Mellins. Humphrey Bogart is thought to be the original Gerber Baby but Bogie would have been twenty-eight years old when Gerber was founded in 1927. Bogart was born on Christmas Day in 1899 and died of esophageal cancer on January 14, 1957. The cigarettes that contributed to Bogart's grainy voice probably contributed to his grainy death. He attended Phillips Academy.

Mellins was located at 40-41 Central Wharf in Boston in an area now occupied by The New England Aquarium. Mellins was established in 1867 and produced one product that was a blend of cow's milk, wheat flour, malt flour, and bicarbonate of potash.

Gerber initially introduced five products and already had national distribution through Daniel Gerber's Fremont Canning Company. Gerber Baby Foods immediate success severely impacted Mellins' sales. Gerber now has around 190 different baby foods.

In 1931 Mead Johnson introduced Pablum, which contained wheat, oatmeal, corn meal, bone meal, yeast, alfalfa leaf, iron, minerals, and vitamins A, B, B2, D and E. The superior Pablum product was another nail in Mellins' coffin.

The Mellins' 1945 comeback attempt really didn't stand a chance. Even pictures of John A. MacLean and nineteen other beautiful babies couldn't revive Mellins. While Gerber

and Beech Nut are commonly recognized,
Mellins remains a mere footnote.

CULTURE SHOCK

I entered Reading schools in the ninth
grade. Although the ninth grade was high school,
our class was split between Parker Junior High
and Coolidge Junior High our freshman year.
Those who attended Coolidge were the first to
graduate from the brand new school. There were
so many post war babies that we overwhelmed
the school system.

My family rented a decent medium grey
house on Lowell Street and we had a pale yellow
1960 Oldsmobile 98 so we were able to pass as
respectable. My mother was a secretary for a
government contracts company and her husband,
Cecil-the-moron, worked in Lynn,
Massachusetts as a dock worker for a camera
retailer. Cecil-the-moron gave himself the title of
"head of shipping" but, in reality, he loaded
trucks and earned squat. My mother carried the
household financially.

Jack was one of my first friends in Reading. Compared to me, Jack was rich. Although Jack was smart and had a supportive family he was always put in the group with what would now be called "special needs" classes. Students who would be diagnosed as ADD, ADHD or learning disabled today, were not given needed support in the 1960s. The students' parents were told, "He/she doesn't apply herself or he is lazy". Since I was in the College Prep Program and Jack was in Shop Classes, we never had any classes together.

Jack's being stuck with the "shop kids" in high school would leave a serious impact on him for his whole life. Some newspaper articles called Jack a genius but I think that title is exaggerated. He was not dumb and he most certainly was cleaver, but I never pegged him as a genius.

Because Jack had a stomach ulcer he was allowed to leave class and get milk in the cafeteria whenever his ulcer bothered him. Jack left classes a lot and would be absent for longer periods than necessary. Jack would wander the halls and peek into classrooms.

We played game was called, Kick-the-Car, but the name is a bit misleading. We really did not kick cars, but rather, we kicked a football to purposely hit cars that were driving on Jack's street.

"Comin'," Jack would yell.

As Jack predicted a car would drive down the street toward Jack's house. We could not see the car because of Jack's house and trees that blocked our view. From half way down his driveway, Jack kicked a football from a "T". The football flew towards the street, careened off the car's hood, scaring the driver but it did no damage. The idea was to not only hit the car with the football but also to shock the driver. If the car was damaged it was judged that the car should not have been going so fast.

"Sorry, sorry. I didn't kick the ball strait," was a typical apology to the driver of the kicked car.

"Is everyone alright?" the shook up lady driver wanted to know.

"Everybody's fine," Jack exclaimed as he picked up the football. "Even the ball is good," he added as he twirled the football in his hands.

"Poor old bat. They should have big signs on their cars that say OLD."

The old bat had not yet turned 50.

Everyone was older than we were back then. Baseball players, police, teachers, doctors (most of whom were white males) and lawyers seemed centuries older than us. Now all professionals are of various ethnicities and are younger than we are. All but professional baseball teams have female members.

Jack could time a car's arrival better than any of us. He also could hear the car coming from further away than the rest of us. His eyes and ears worked exceptionally well and he had very good coordination.

The final kick occurred one fall afternoon around 5:00 PM. A Buick Electra drove slowly down Hanscom Avenue with all of the cars windows open. It was a glorious sunny day with the maple trees on the street vibrant in yellows, oranges, and reds. The driver lived towards the end of the street. He always worked around his yard and always waved to us kids; even chatted at times. Not only was the Bucik's driver a pleasant gentleman but Jack remembered that he gave out great Halloween candy. Mr. Waldron's wife was sickly and housebound.

Mr. Waldron's house was between Jack's house and the road to school. Sometimes on his way home from school Mr. Waldron would talk briefly to Jack.

"How'd school go today?"

"Good. Your lawn looks great."

"I try."

"How's your wife Mr. Waldron?"

"Oh, I think she's getting better. She's got something called Alzheimer's but she's better today."

"Tell her I said hi."

"Study hard so that you can become an engineer."

The only engineer that Jack could envision was a train engineer. "Why would I want to become like Choo Choo Charlie?" Jack wondered.

Jack kicked, the ball soared through the Buick's window, and ended in the back seat of the car. The poor old guy was so shaken that he couldn't catch his breath. Jack assured him again and again that everything was fine. Ed brought the guy some water from the hose. The guy was shaken but able to continue on home.

Jack and Ed looked at each other but both knowing what had to be done.

"That's it. We're done. Nobody but nobody could ever better that kick," Jack boasted. We never played Kick-the Car again.

Our Kick-the-Car game did not gain world wide acceptance. Go figure.

THE MATURATION OF RMHS 65

In 1947 and 1948, when the graduating class of RMHS 1965 were born, our mothers held us tightly during our first trip in an automobile. Some mothers may have sat in the back seat to protect us as we were transported home from our birth hospital. Mom held us as securely as a mother could. There were no child carriers back then. Cars did not have seat belts either - not even lap belts. Hand made leather lap belts were sometimes used in open top race cars to keep drivers from being thrown out of the car upon rollover, but car manufacturers had not yet installed them in passenger cars.

As Mom held us tightly as she admired our beautiful face and counted out ten fingers and toes one more time. Lap seat belts, padded dashboards, seat belts with shoulder straps, child carriers, booster seats and air bags would all come later.

No longer manufactured, the Nash Rambler was the first car to install seat belts as a standard item in 1957. The advent of nylon webbing enabled the manufacture of uniformly made, secure seat belts, that would eventually be installed in all cars sold in America. Disc brakes became standard in 1964 and rear facing child seats were introduced the same year. Windshield defrosters were finally introduced as standard items when we were six years old.

It's amazing that any of us made it from that first car trip to graduation eighteen years later.

In the 1960s, employees smoked in their offices, on the train, at work, in restaurants, and on airplanes. Nonsmokers were forced to tolerate the smokers back then.

Many of Reading Municipal High School class of 1965 graduates (RMHS65ers) were the second or third child of post WW II parents. We are referred to as Baby Boomers. Dad came home from WW II, mom still looked good = children.

Divorce was fairly rare in our early years and was considered a blemish. Illegal drugs existed but were unheard of in Reading. Alcohol was available in high school; some of us used it and some abused it. During summer weekends, high schoolers could be found drinking six packs at night, on the hill overlooking eight lane Route 93 . Rippa, the town drunk, from Woburn, was most often used for procuring beer for us minors. Beer was what we chose. GIQs (Giant Imperial Quarts) were the cheapest.

In first and second grade we hid under our desks when air raid sirens sounded. We covered our faces with our hands. Our desks, we were told, would help protect us from the effects of a nuclear bomb. A sample bomb shelter, built of concrete blocks, was built behind the Reading town library. Vandals quickly took it over and covered the floor with broken beer bottles.

We had lived through a great deal of change. We were born before television came to the masses. In 1948, there were 350,000 TVs in America. When we did get TV it was black and white. Televisions received only three channels (seven in Los Angeles). Channels had to be changed by getting up and turning the dial and adjusting the antennae. There was no such thing as a clear crisp picture in early days of TV. TV stations broadcast for only 42 hours per week. At 8:00 pm the stations went off the air and a test pattern came on.

By 1959 color TV came to market for big bucks and remote control was soon added.

Many families did not get a color TV until their black and white set broke. The one million per year mark, in color TV sales, did not get reached until 1964. In 1948 only 10% of the population had ever seen a TV. It was magic.

In 1950 a 3 inch screen "Pilot" brand, black and white, TV cost $100.00, while a 20 inch "DuMont" brand cost $2,495.00 (the equivalent of $28,000.00 today). Gasoline cost $.26 per gallon, bread $.14 per loaf, a postage stamp was $.03 and the Dow Jones Industrial Average was at 177 (the Dow closed at 17,425.03 on 12/31/15). By 1959 42 million Americans had TV.

The World Wide Web was not invented until we were forty-one years old. Google launched when we were fifty.

Telephones were around when we were born - telephones with switchboards were used since 1878. Early telephone numbers had only three and then four digits in the whole telephone number. Later seven digits came into play with letters (which were really a transposed numbers) like MUrrayhill 5-4321 or MU5-4321 but it was really 685-4321. Area codes, which came much later, allowed direct dialing for long distance calls, so that the user did not need to use an operator. Yes, an operator was needed for each long distance call in the old days.

Today operators no longer exist at all. Early telephones had a round dial with ten holes into which the caller inserted his/her finger to rotate the dial. One would dial the number zero for an operator - not the letter o(perator), which is really number 6. Of course one no longer "dials" but the term still lingers. Dialing "0" will no longer get an operator but rather a recording that might instruct the user to dial 911 if there is an emergency. Siri wasn't even an apple in Steve Job's eye in our early years. Even Steven Jobs didn't exist until 1955.

In the early days all but the rich had party lines. Party lines consisted of groups of families that shared the same line. All the families that shared a party line had different telephone numbers but the phone still rang at all the partys' homes. Each home had a differently numbered ring and since party lines had 2 and 4 families, customers had to be attentive. First the phone would ring one long ring, as an alert, then the individual party's code, 1-4 rings. Young children would sometimes pick up the phone whenever it rang - as did the drunk, the elderly, and inattentive. The system was lacking at best.

Early telephones actually had two little bells inside that a striker would hit making a ringing sound. British blokes still use the term "ring you up". Cell phones can be programmed to make a ringing sound similar to the old bells. New ringing sounds are made by tiny little people inside the cell phones.

If one family was using the party line a different party family could pick up and listen in on the conversation. If one party talked too long and another party family member wanted/needed to use the phone, the needy party would pick up the phone frequently and groan into the receiver. If there was an emergency the user was required to give up the line - not everyone did and on occasion tragedies were exacerbated.

Sometimes a whole telephone network would be so overburdened that the destination number was unattainable. "The lines are full" was heard all too frequently. There was no privacy. Homeland Security would not be needed if the old party line system was still in effect.

In 1959 telephone rates were $3.25 per month for a four party line, $3.80 for a two party line and $4.40 for a private line. In house "extensions" were an additional $1.00. Taxes were an additional 10%. The very rich had an additional "children's phone" with a separate number.

Minimum wage in 1945 - 1949 when the RMHS65ers were born, was $.40/hour. By 1959 minimum wage had increased to $1.00/hour. Before 1938 there was no minimum wage.

Undreamed of features like answering machines, call forwarding, call waiting and computer modems would not come for decades. By 1969 10% of the US population still didn't have telephones. Cell phones would appear even later. By 2002 most phones in the world were cell phones.

In 1956 people actually tried to get racially segregated party lines. Segregated party lines were denied by the AT&T division of The Bell System. Ma Bell, as it was called, had a total vertical monopoly on the telephone business.

Bell owned the phone lines, Bell manufactured the phones, they owned all the phones in people's homes (use of their phones was paid monthly), only Bell employees could install the phones and lines. Bell owned all the telephone booths, long distance, and calls had to channel through Bell's system. Bell even had a monopoly on the Yellow Pages. If a family owned only one common stock it most likely would have been Bell. Bell stock was considered as solid as the dollar.

If a household wanted an extension line, a Bell employee was required to install it and only a Bell telephone could be used. Eventually people "acquired" phones and installed them themselves. Self installers faced misdemeanor charges for the installations and theft charges for having an unauthorized phone.

On January 8, 1982 Bell Systems signed a consent decree that split the Bell System into separate companies thus ending its monopoly. The previously vertically integrated Bell System ceased to be the biggest corporation in American history after its actual split in 1984.

Reading High School athletics were very competitive. There was a great deal of respect among classmates but competition was freakishly high, especially in sports. In the 9th grade, if one didn't get 100% on President Kennedy's physical fitness test that person would be compelled to lie and attest to getting 100%.

While we were in high school the football team won every game for four years. The basketball team attended playoffs all four years. Our classmate Kippy played varsity baseball all four years.

If one didn't get his (I don't know about

the girls) drivers license on the first try it was a major embarrassment. Cars were a major factor in our lives. We simply loved them.

Driving a car to school, especially driving one's own car (not one's mother's station wagon) created high status. No one bicycled. No one.

Unlike proms today, we went as different sex couples only and odd numbered groups were unheard of. No same sex couples ever attended a single prom while we attended RMHS. In fact same sex couples would not have been allowed to attend proms. There was a lot of pressure for some to find an acceptable date. Today's youth are much more open and flexible. That's a good thing.

After college we adhered to a similar competitive state. What college did we attend? What grades did we get? First jobs and pay scales were compared. Some of us exaggerated (lied).

Then things changed. Eventually no one gave a rat's ass about what kind of car one drove or how many bedrooms and baths we had. Our children became our focus and eventually, of course, our grandchildren. Our health was frequently talked about. We seemed to have a lot of "procedures". Some of us died which saddened us. There were always pictures of our classmates who died, laid out at every reunion and function our class had.

We developed a more genuine caring. We loved each other - for the most part. Assholes were still ass holes but we became more tolerant of them. Old grudges were forgotten. In short, we matured.

JACK-the-BAD

Both Jack and his younger sister were adopted. Jack was spoiled with material things but his sister was not. I realized that their parents would brag: "This is my son, see what (material possessions) he's got. This is my daughter, see how smart she is".

In the ninth grade Jack got a go-cart. Use of his go-cart was limited to the family driveway. The driver would go towards the driveway's street entrance as fast as possible, turn the steering wheel until it locked so that the cart would spin, turning it 180 degrees, then the driver would accelerate back towards the garage, where a regular turn could be made, then accelerate back towards the street. Repeat and repeat again. Since Jack's driveway was the only track available, use of the cart was extremely limited, until Jack (only Jack) would drive it up and down the street. Too much street driving would summon the police.

"Have you kids been driving that go-cart in the street?" was usually the police question.

"We just went on the street when we spun out," would be the regular response.

"Well don't let it go out into the street."

Driving the go-cart in the street was a cat and mouse game. Jack and the police knew that the driver had to be caught in the act. The police had better things to do than chase a go-cart. Besides, the police would have done exactly the same thing when they were young. Eventually the neighbors stopped calling the police out of frustration. Jack's go-cart capers were probably his introduction to how police think about crime and how to not have your go-cart taken away.

Jack learned that:

.Being polite to the police goes a long way. Talk to the police. They might even divulge who ratted you out for driving in the street.

.When you sell your go-cart, you can egg the rat across the street's house. It was done.

.Coming from a comfortable, well respected family goes a long way.

.Lying to police is allowed; just make sure that the lies are believable and that the police can cover their asses with their superiors.

.Police really don't care about petty crap. Don't hurt anyone and make sure that the go-cart's muffler isn't too loud .

.Even the police don't like whiny neighbors.

I never once saw John, Jack's adopted father do anything with Jack. He never threw the football around, never played catch, and never worked on any of Jack's car projects with him.

Ed's father was the best. Joe and Ed built

and raced a hydroplane, Joe showed Ed how to work on cars, and gave him advise on how to be a good human being. Ed has had one wife and been the most financially successful of our group.

Jack's father, Hank, did little with Jack in high school but Hank was not a handy guy. In his earlier years Hank would play catch with Jack.

My Dad was a good guy but stopped visiting me a couple of years after he and my mother divorced. He taught me how to build stone walls and how to use a wood plane. My Dad was a wonderful man.

Fathers make a difference.

OTHER FRIENDS - JACK-THE-GOOD AND ED (ALSO GOOD)

All the girls from RMHS65 loved Jack-the-Good - all of them. JacktG just had a easy, naturally fun way about him. And yes, of course he was handsome. He always held hands when he was with a girl. He made the girls feel special because, to JacktG, they were special.

Jack-t-G never actually made an appearance at Greystone where we have reunions every year. In fact he never even saw the place. After high school he joined the Marines and went to Vietnam. He did return from Vietnam but in a body bag. Greystone would not be acquired by Bob for thirty-five years.

JacktG, Ed and I were best friends. Jack MacLean was a peripheral friend. Ed and I, some fifty-five years later, are still good friends. Ed is the tallest of the four and was voted the handsomest guy in our class. Ed is dark complected and still a good looking guy. JacktG, was of Irish/German decent with a medium complexion. He was voted class poet and his rock band played "Loui Loui" at the class talent show. Jack MacLean was also a very good looking guy. I am blond and not bad looking but not as good looking as Ed, JacktG nor Jack MacLean. Trying to be honest here.

I don't remember how we got to be

friends and actually we were not inseparable friends but all four were adventurous and not afraid to break rules.

JacktG lived with his parents and younger brother Jimmy in a 3 bedroom white painted brick house on a pleasant street in Reading. Hank, Jack's dad, was a "detail man" (salesman) for a large drug company. His mother worked in a doctor's office. The family was comfortable but not wealthy by Reading standards.

Ed lived in a nice part of town but his house was a modest ranch. Ed's brother was is also a very bright guy and his sister was gorgeous.

Since neither Jack-the-Good nor I were particularly good students we played hooky. We played hooky a lot. Our favorite destinations were the beaches of Massachusetts North Shore. Crane's Beach in Ipswich, Wingaersheek Beach in Gloucester and Singing Beach in Manchester were our haunts. Singing Beach is called so named because of the sound that can be made by scuffing one's feet along the sand. The mansions overlooking the beach are gorgeous. We were determined to be successful enough to own a great mansion.

Until I got my first car, a 1954 Ford, we would hitchhike to wherever we wanted to go. Senior year I was "sick" for 43 days days. Ed did not skip school as much as Jack and I. That might have contributed to Ed's getting admitted to Tufts, my only getting admitted to Suffolk University and Jack's merely getting admitted to a community college - where he decided not even to enroll. College was never an option for Jack MacLean.

My old Ford was a murky dark green four door. It did have a small V-8 engine (the first year Ford made a real V-8 - not a flathead 8). The car had been converted to a three speed floor shift that I could shift with my right foot. Ed and Jack thought that my foot shifting was pretty cool. Gas was around $.25/gallon in the mid 60s. The car ran and ran. I never changed the oil and never did any maintenance. I had no money. I ended up giving the car to classmate Lenny.

After high school Jack worked in a

plastics factory in Wakefield before joining the marines. He pledged to either come back from Viet Nam a national hero or to not come back alive.

Being extremely smart didn't hurt Ed's admission to Tufts. Ed worked for several very large computer companies and eventually became president of one companies' super computer division. Ed was able to retire at 49 years old.

On Christmas Eve in 1964 Dave, Jack-the-Good, Ed and I went to see the James Bond movie Goldfinger. We went in my Ford along a dark windy back road to Ipswich, Massachusetts. Dave suggested that we take a slight detour in order to show us something interesting. The thing of interest was a mansion set in the back of a field. The place had never been completed. We pretty much just viewed the immense place from the road then proceeded to Ipswich. Goldfinger was our first James Bond movie and we all loved it.

The day after Christmas JacktG and I went back to "The Mansion". We parked about a half mile away in order not to arouse attention. Vandals (we were not vandals we were adventurers) had entered from the back so we did the same. The place was huge inside with rooms the size of which we had never seen. There was an elevator shaft but no elevator.

Vandals had trashed the place strewing the contents of the dozens and dozens of trunks and furniture that had been stored there. The elevator shaft had been filled with the storage trunks and their contents. We found many books, some leather bound, tweed sports coats, tuxes and tails. Much of the furniture had been smashed. We left with some of the books.

Of course we returned a few days later and a few days after that. On one of the last days we ventured up to the third floor which was much less vandalized. Jack found books to his heart's content. He found a tweed houndstooth sports coat that he absolutely loved. I still have the coat over half a century later.

After I opened one steamer trunk, I called out, "Jack. Jack come quickly".

JacktG thought that I had found a body.

What I had found was a trunk full of silver. Tea settings and platters; some plate and some sterling.

We stashed our find under the Mineral Street bridge near Jack's house sincerely hoping that no one else would stumble upon it.

Since the statute of limitations has long since expired, I guess that I can own up to our selling the silver. Note: plated silver is nearly worthless and sterling silver is worth about a twentieth of gold.

The mansion was razed long ago, never having been completed. There was a rumor that a series of people had owned the place, all of whom died prematurely. I'm sure that we could have completed the mansion if given a chance. We were infallible.

JacktG was a very good ice hockey player and was on the varsity team since entering high school. The Reading players had to play and practice at the Lynn Arena, miles away. The inconvenient practices were sometimes held at 4 or 5:00 am so dedication to the sport was a must. Eventually Jack had it with the disturbing schedule and quit the team his senior year.

"I quit hockey yesterday," Jack told me.

Knowing that hockey was Jack's ticket to college and scholarships I sternly responded, "You can't quit."

"Yes I can and I did."

"Jack you know . . ."

"LET IT GO."

The Vietnam war was raging with half a million American soldiers fighting. Fifty thousand young Americans would die needlessly taking, losing and retaking hills with hard to pronounce names. Since the major deferment to the draft was college, college enrollment became an absolute necessity. I knew that if my friend didn't enroll in college that he would probably get drafted and that he would have a one in ten chance of being killed in a country that most of us had previously never heard of.

Draft numbers were chosen by a birth date lottery. A low number, without deferment, insured being drafted. Jack's draft number was twenty-two. Knowing that Jack had a low military draft number sent a chill over me.

Quitting hockey was akin to Jack's tearing up his ticket to happiness and possibly his life.

Jack's name is on the Vietnam War Memorial. His picture is at every RMHS65 function. I swear that ALL the girls in high school were in love with him, including some of the teachers.

ROSCOE JAMES MACLEAN

Roscoe James MacLean was a nickname that Jack-the-Good gave Jack MacLean. None of us seems to know where the name came from. I guess that it just popped into JacktG's head one day.

"Roscoe" is underworld term for a gun.

Jack was a fast runner. He could sprint and could run long distances as fast as anyone on the cross country team. Jack knew that he could outrun most cops, who wore leather shoes in the 1960s, since he wore sneakers and could sprint.

Jack also knew that Reading police never ever fired their guns. Most Reading police never removed their guns from their holsters except for target practice. If he needed to run from a crime Jack would most likely be able to get away. Jack actually never had to run from the Reading police but he knew that he could if necessary.

Jack lived less than half a mile away from my house. Easy walking distance. I sometimes walked around Reading just to feel the beauty of the town.

One day, I walked by Jack's house and saw that Jack had a new red go-cart. I walked by the go-carters because I was not yet friends with Jack. I yearned to give that cart a try. It looked like a great deal of fun. I walked slowly so that the three guys could see me and possibly call me over to participate. They didn't. Possibly there were too many of them there already sharing the one cart.

Jack's next motor vehicle was a Honda 50. Since Jack was two years older than I was, he got his driver's license in the tenth grade. Having a "nearly" motorcycle in the tenth grade was piss hot. Jack removed the exhaust baffle soon after he got it. The Honda, with the baffle removed sounded like a loud, angry wasp.

Jack rarely let anyone ride on the back because the extra weight caused the Honda to be too slow - power to weight ratio. I remember seeing Jack buzz up the hill next to Reading High School. Jack and the Honda displayed the freedom of a hawk and, quite frankly, the noise added to the image that the Honda and he displayed.

I walked home with my books in my arms. Jack never carried books with him. He never studied or did homework. He didn't care because he was going to fail his tests anyway.

Jack traded the Honda for an blue MGA. Of all Jack's vehicles I loved the MGA the most. Jack told his aunt that he loved the Honda 50 but he really couldn't take a girl with him and that using it in bad weather and in the winter wasn't practical. Jack had the MGA all picked out and a two seat car apparently made sense to his aunt so she bought it for him. I got to ride in the MGA quite a bit since Jack and I had gotten to be better friends and the car could hold two people. Sometimes neither Jack nor I knew where we were going when we rode in the MGA but we didn't care. The car was so much fun.

One summer afternoon we went to Rye, New Hampshire. We went to check out the beach huts since Jack was trying to find a girl from Winchester that he wanted to hook up with. Jack confided that the girl's father absolutely hated him. The father may have even had a restraining order against Jack, since the daughter was under the age of consent.

I realize now that we were really stalking the girl.

We never found the girl from Winchester although we looked for her all afternoon. We didn't leave Rye until well after dark.

Since the car looked better with the top down, Jack almost never put the top up. The ride back to Reading was cold with the top down. Jack was pissed when a car passed us.

"Shit!" Jack exclaimed as he hit the steering wheel.

"What's the matter?" I asked.

"He passed me."

"So?"

"I don't like to be passed."

Competitive was our middle name.

MGAs are really fun cars despite their terrible electrics. The MGA's 1588 cc engine had only 79 horsepower but with aluminum hood trunk and doors they weighed a mere 1988 pounds so the power to weight ratio was adequate. The car's canvas top was a nightmare to put down and much worse to put up. The plastic side windows came off and could be stored in the boot (trunk for you nonAnglophiles). The wire wheels are also problematic but they are beautiful. If I had an MGA when I was in high school I would have slept in it I loved them so much. But I digress.

I never asked to drive the MGA because I knew that "no" would have been Jack's response. Jack always drove.

Then, senior year, Jack traded the MGA for a black Corvette. Again, given to him by his aunt. I only rode in the Corvette once and remember liking the MGA much more. By the time Jack got the Corvette I had my own car. My 1954 Ford wasn't nearly as cool as any of Jack's vehicles but I got to drive and I love to drive.

Jack's family had an in-ground pool installed the summer after our high school graduation. Almost nobody had in-ground pools in New England back then. Pools became more prolific with the advent of vinyl pool liners, which are cheaper and easier to maintain than Gunnite.

Before Jack's family got their pool I had literally never seen a residential pool. To my virgin pool eyes, an in-ground domestic pool was the richest thing in the world. Someday, I promised myself, I would have an in-ground pool. And, yes, I have a pool.

Jack's family's pool has since been filled in and the space made into parking spaces. There is a spruce tree growing in what used to be the pool's shallow end. The spruce is about six inches in diameter - about twelve years old.

I wasn't actually jealous of Jack; maybe envious but I didn't want what he had, I just wanted things like he had.

Jack was 6'2" tall, slim, with swept back blond hair and bright blue eyes. Eventually many women remembered his very blue eyes. He was a handsome young man. He had a pock marked face but I never thought it looked all that bad. In the right (wrong?) light the pock marks looked more discernible.

In high school Jack never had a girlfriend and never went to a prom. When he went to a school dance he only stayed for a short time. Jack liked girls, in fact he liked them a lot, but the relationship had to be on Jack's terms. Jack especially liked to stalk girls.

All of Jack's friends outside of school were smart. He never hung around with the students from the shop classes.

I sat next to Jack at graduation. Our high school principal Dr. Karakasian, who was a wonderful man, spoke. He stated sadly, that it was sad that after graduation some of us would never read another book. Jack responded to me by saying, "I never read a book in high school either."

Jack's world was a narrowly focused one. While he could probably recount who the President of the United States was, he would never know the name of a US senator. He might know the name of the vice president but would never know who was secretary of state. He would know the engine displacement and horsepower of many cars, domestic and foreign, but the name of any author or the creator of famous paintings would be totally alien to him.

Jack's favorite subjects, as depicted in RMHS65 yearbook (called the Pioneer), were "lunch and girls". He never played any organized sport, was never a member of any club, nor did he play any instrument in high school. Jack didn't get in fights and left the "taken" girls alone. According to the Pioneer, Jack wanted to attend an Aero-tech school after graduation.

Jack despised smoking, drinking and drug use and I never saw him even try any. The aversion may have come from his parents, who I never saw drink or smoke. We never talked about it.

Once a girl Jack was talking to, while standing outside her car at Reading's train depot, removed a cigarette from a pack and lit it.

"Throw that thing away," Jack demanded.

"It's MY cigarette," she said defensively, knowing that Jack detested smoking.

"They're evil."

"Unlike you, the white things I put in my mouth are clean and come in a pack."

Jack grabbed the lit cigarette from her mouth, threw it on the ground as he pushed his body against hers with her back to her car.

"I ought to screw you right here."

"Do it," she replied, calling his bluff.

He didn't.

Jack's family and my family attended Reading's Episcopal, Church of the Good Shepard. Both families attended very infrequently. Jack never talked about God, Jesus, Satan or religion.

Jack was always well dressed and well groomed yet he had no desire to dress stylishly. Once he noticed that I had worn the same shirt two days in a row and told me to never, never wear the same shirt for two days. It was as if I had committed a Cardinal Sin. In the GQ sense he was, of course, correct.

Jack's cars were always immaculate inside and out. After washing and waxing his car Jack would give the vehicle a coat of Lemon Pledge. His car had to be the shiniest and even smell good on the outside. To characterize Jack as compulsive would be an understatement.

Jack always treated his cars like children. He not only kept them immaculate, he diligently changed the oil every three thousand miles, greased them and always used Mobil premium gas. He almost always filled up at Charlie's Mobil on Main Street in Reading which, conveniently, was next to McDonalds.

One day, as Jack sat waiting at Charlie's Mobile for his gas tank to be filled, he observed the gas attendant (gas station attendants back then pumped gas and checked the oil for customers). The attendant showed the driver the dipstick that indicated that he was "down a quart". Then the attendant took what appeared to Jack to be an empty oil can (oil came in quart cans), inserted the spout into the can, and appeared to put oil into the car. The attendant held his hand over the hole in the bottom of the can to obscure that the can had been used and drained previously. Dan, the attendant, then threw the can away into the trash.

"What a beautiful scam," thought Jack. Insert the dipstick partially in so that it indicates that the car needs oil and then pretend to add from the empty can. The attendant, of course, would then pocket the money paid for the oil.

Jack parked his car, pulled out the can with holes in each end out of the trash and confronted Dan. Dan knew that if Jack told Charlie he would be fired. Dan had a wife and a baby and needed the job.

Jack started to laugh. "You sleazy little bastard."

Jack displayed the can with the holes at both ends. Dan was busted and scared.

"I never would have thought of this. I really like the part where you show the guy the dipstick."

"Come over here," Dan walked to a drum of grease.

Dan stirred the grease, put his head into the barrel, and breathed deeply again and again.

Soon Dan felt a rush.

"What are you doing?" Jack asked.

"Huffing."

"Why?"

"It gives me a buzz."

Dan stirred the grease barrel and once more breathed the mind numbing fumes.

Jack took his turn huffing at the grease vapors. He too liked the rush and the toxic buzz.

Neither guy realized the damage that huffing could cause but both liked the high. Dan let Jack use the garage's lift whenever he wanted after that and both guys huffed grease on a regular basis.

For a short time Jack had a 1955 Chevy. He replaced the car's front seats with Rambler seats. Rambler seats could be reclined to make the car's interior into a flat bed. He also installed a condom dispenser. These particular condoms came on a long roll which was kept under the front seat. The condoms were fed inside the door channel so that they could be dispensed through the headliner near the driver.

Jack had a fixation for anything latex. He

especially liked condoms. Latex gloves eventually became necessary in his profession.

Jack didn't keep the Chevy long because he disliked the four door sedan and really wanted a two door coupe. The Chevy had an old original radio. One Florida newspaper reported that Jack always tinkered with radios even as a child. That report was patently untrue. Jack never had a walkie talkie, a ham radio, nor did he have a police radio while in high school.

Jack's adopted father John owned a small business that sold newspaper advertising to businesses. The business was successful enough to afford a Reading class lifestyle. As Jack used to say, "My father sells square inches."

I never liked John's mustache. The pencil thin, Errol Flynn, mustache was terribly over groomedand always appearing to have had extreme attention to keep it perfect. And it was always perfect, never too long or too wide. It was always exactly the same every time I saw it. By 1965 John's mustache was turning grey.

In the summer John slept in the small trailer that served as a pool house. No one but

John was ever allowed inside the little trailer. Either John would be inside with the door bolted or he was outside with the door padlocked. Even Jack never figured out a way to break in. John was neither Clark Gable hansom (although he had a Clark Gable style mustache) nor Elephant Man ugly.

John had an elevated status among other Reading residents because he started and ran his own business. Being self employed was not rampant in the 1960s. Those who worked for corporations envied those who could make it on their own. The independence of being one's own boss was very appealing especially to men who had a regular job and a boss. To create a business out of nothing was considered a great accomplishment.

The only meals that I ever ate at Jack's house were outside, cooked on the grill. We generally had steak, corn on the cob and egg potato salad.

Jack and I would sometimes listen to Frank Sinatra records in Jack's bedroom. He particularly liked "My Way". I like Sinatra too.

Once a girl from neighboring Woburn (Woburn was not as nice as Reading) made fun of Jack for listening to Sinatra. "How old are you? Like a hundred," she rebuked. Jack never listened to Frank Sinatra again.

Muriel, Jack's mother, was a Reading wife. She took care of the family home and cared for her children. Muriel never worked in a traditional job in her life. It was John's responsibility to provide for the family. Muriel was overweight and not a pretty woman. Muriel defined herself as being her husband's wife, as many women did in the 1950s and 1960s.

John and Muriel's adopted children came from around the corner not from around the world, as is common now. Jack was rumored to be the son of a married local surgeon and his mistress. Jack was adopted shortly after his birth. Jack's sister was adopted two years later. She was quite smart and pretty. She went to college in Boston, graduated, and married a minister.

Jack always referred to his parents as his mother and father; not as his adoptive parents. For years I didn't even know that Jack and his sister were adopted. Jack always respected his mother, father, aunt and sister, and never spoke an negative thing about any of them.

In the ninth grade the sole of my shoe separated and I was forced to walk by sliding my shoe along the floor so that it wouldn't flap. After about a week my mother decided that it was time to buy new shoes. We went to shoe store that sold seconds and discontinued shoes. Cool shoes, like loafers, were too expensive, so my mother objected, saying that loafers were not sturdy enough. I settled on a pair of ripple sole shoes. The shoes had wedges that went across the bottom. They were "sturdy". And cheap.

The night that I got the new shoes, Jack and I were walking together and I sought his approval of the shoes.

"You know they make me taller." True.

"They give me spring in my step." Also true.

"I think that I can run faster." Questionable.

"They suck. Now shut up," Jack reprimanded.

They did suck and I did shut up.

Winslows was located across the street from the Reading train station. Many high school kids hung out outside Winslows, where we could sit on the flower wall. There was a lot of traffic to watch and passing friends would wave and honk their horns making it, basically, the only location in Reading where you might ever hear a car's horn.

Sometimes the Reading Police would make us leave the area. Sometimes there would be a fist fight but no one used knives or guns. No one bought or sold drugs.

Jack never hung out at Winslows. On a rare occasion he would park across the street at the train station but never mingled with the Winslows crowd. I think that Jack feared that he wouldn't be accepted because he was spoiled. Actually he probably would have been beaten up by guys jealous of his cars.

About a year and a half after we graduated I went to Jack's house. I had not heard from Jack in a long while. Muriel told me that Jack was in Florida running his amusement at a carnival. I was working in the adjudication area of mutual funds department of a Boston bank at the time; a fact that Muriel was apparently aware of. I was dressed in a three piece suit.

"Hi Mrs. MacLean. Do you know Jack's telephone number in Florida?"

"He doesn't have a phone since he travels for his business. He's running his own business in Florida," she boasted.

"You mean the carnival game?"

"Yes, his own business," she bragged, as she shut the door on my face. Muriel apparently did not like my calling Jack's business a game. Since Jack had no telephone we stayed out of touch.

I believe that Muriel thought Jack was making the big bucks with his carnival game. I'm sure that the truth of Jack's burglaries crushed the whole family when Jack was eventually arrested.

Like his father, Jack did have his own business, so his parents were proud. The amusement was absolutely minimally constructed, made up of a rope ladder with wooden steps with the bottom and top attached with only one line so that it would swivel. Walking up the rope looked easier than the actual task. Jack made the ladder look even easier by his being able to ascend and descend facing foreword or backward. He also learned the carny trick of striking the bottom if a climber got close to the top thus knocking the climber off balance and causing the person to fall.

Jack and his wife liked the carnival lifestyle and his amusement provided him with sufficient funds to get by. The couple lived and traveled in a camper going from carnival site to carnival site. The carnival traveled from Miami to Gainsville.

If one of the amusement's participants fell off the rope ladder it was just too bad. People didn't sue so much back then but safety became an issue, so eventually Jack's carnival game was suspended.

Since job options for Jack were slim he was pleased that he had the back up of being a professional burglar. Jack worked diligently at his burglary job.

Carnivals attracted people who can't find employment in mainstream society. Carnivals attracted ex-convicts, substance abusers, and other outliers. Jack fit right in. The itinerant lifestyle enabled the dodgy carnival people to be one step ahead of anyone who might be looking for them. The lifestyle was an especially beneficial lifestyle for anyone who was trying to evade the law. Jack befriended carnies who had committed crimes and knew the ropes.

Jack learned how to bypass home security systems, learned how to steal cars, learned how to open safes, and pick locks. Jack was amazed at how easy it was to circumvent locks, security, and stay ahead of the law.

A device called a "slim jim" enables a lock smith, or a car thief, to open a locked car in seconds. Slim Jims were as common in carnivals as screw drivers. Jack practiced opening locked cars with his slim jim and got so proficient that he was faster than his instructor. Jack bought lock smith tools from an old carnival worker who hadn't used the tools in years.

Jack was a very likable guy. He

befriended professional thieves who he knew could teach him nefarious tricks. A lonely professional locksmith showed Jack tricks of the trade and gave him books that only professionals had access to. Many people like to show off their knowledge and Jack found and capitalized on those pedantic people.

Pickins has been describes as crazy, a loner, a heathen, and antisocial. He was only forty five but he looked sixty-five. All his life he was skinny as a rail; thus his nick name which came from country actor Slim Pickins. Slim Pickins died on December 8, 1983 - Jack's thirty-seventh birthday.

Pickins never smiled or greeted anyone. He was a true curmudgeon. For some reason he liked Jack.

Pickins had a scruffy black beard and always wore a soiled blue pork pie hat. Pickins had the same hat for twenty-three years. It blew off while he was on Jack's speed boat and quickly sunk - probably because it was so weighted down with dirt.

Pickins did know how to break into

homes. He was skilled at lock picking, could disable security alarms, knew how to cheat at poker, could break into cars and hot wire them, and he knew when to walk away.

Pickins ran the Tilt-a-whirl at the carnival yet he lived better than he should have on an ride operator's salary. He bought a new Dodge Ram pickup every two years, he had the second nicest camper of all the carnival employees, and he had his pride and joy Harley Davidson.

Pickins was able to drive the Harley despite his having blown off his left hand. Many years earlier Pickins had to wait for a pay phone. After he put in his money in the slot, the operator told him to deposit "forty more cents". He had just gotten to the phone and had deposited his one and only dime. The operator told him that he sounded just like the previous user who owed the forty cents and cut him off for not paying. Pickins' plea was for service ignored. Ma Bell could do things like that because she had a total monopoly on the telephone system. In fact, Ma Bell pissed a lot of people off.

Pickins was livid and promised revenge. He vowed to damage Ma Bell far more than his loss of ten cents. He made six pipe bombs and managed to blow up five telephone booths. While setting the fuse for the sixth, it exploded prematurely, leaving Pickins unable to clap his hands ever again. Pickins hand was replaced with a pinching hook.

Pickins was able to drive his Harley by clutching, braking, and accelerating with his right hand. Jack gained Pickins friendship by admiring his adaptability.

"How do you drive that thing?" asked Jack.

"Simple. I moved the clutch leaver to the right side."

"But how do you crank the throttle and clutch at the same time?"

"I twist the throttle with my thumb and let out the clutch leaver with my four fingers," Pickins boasted.

"Can I try?"

"Nope."

Pickins had burgled homes for three

decades but he robbed infrequently and randomly. He never got caught so Jack figured that burglary was an undetectable crime. Actually only 10% of burglaries are solved. Burglary is generally a low priority for police since most people are reimbursed through insurance.

Pickins only burgled homes when he was desperate - like badly needing a down payment for his Harley. Pickins had been to jail for six months for assault and never wanted to return to jail. Jack convinced him to rob a house together.

Jack and Pickins staked out and robbed a house in West Palm Beach. Jack immediately saw that he could improve on Pickins' style:

. The take from their robbery of the modest residences was meager. Why not rob wealthier homes where there would be more to steal?

. Pickins robbed homes barehanded, so he had to take time to wipe down any surfaces that he touched. Why not use latex gloves and simply not leave fingerprints at all?

. During one robbery, Pickins took a

television. The TV was cumbersome and only netted $25.00. Stealing the TV didn't make sense to Jack.

. Pickins took any and all jewelry. Why not take just the gold? The worthless jewelry had to be disposed of, could be found by the authorities, and possibly traced.

. Pickins picked the West Palm house entry lock. Why not make a key earlier enabling a faster entrance for a break in? A picked lock leaves obvious marks.

Fortunately for Jack, Pickins was not afraid to fence hot goods. By fencing for Jack Pickins made enough money to buy a house, retire from the carnival business and live happily ever after.

Jack loved to plan and think through every burglary scenario again and again. Jack felt that robbing people's homes and evading the law showed his superior intellect. Thorough planning helped make Jack a successful burglar.

RESIDENCE #1

Jack was ready to try his first solo robbery but first he had to find an appropriate house to rob. He drove and drove around Palm Beach but realized that the residences were too big and scary for an attempt. West Palm Beach didn't have enough wealth and Palm Beach was too wealthy. Jack tried a different tack.

Plan A

Jack entered the office of Mathews and Wolf Real Estate in Palm Beach. The office was impressive with its cherry paneled walls, thick carpeting, and beautiful receptionist. He had not called ahead and the office was not used to cold call walk ins. Jack, in fact, did not have a telephone due to the carnivals itinerant life style. The receptionist greeted Jack warmly anyway.

"Im Jack," he announced with with an out reached hand.

"Maryanne," the receptionist responded as she shook his hand. Maryanne was young and pretty. Her light brown hair had a french braid and her short skirt showed off her killer legs.

"How may I help you?"

"I'm in the market."

Another beautiful woman arrived introducing herself, "Susie. What can I do for you Jack?"

Susie had been with Mathews and Wolf for just a year but was an immediate success in real estate sales.

"I'm looking for a 4 or 5 bedroom with 3 or 4 baths on a canal."

"Come into my office and we'll see what we've got."

Susie's office was a cubicle without a window. Both Susie and Jack sized each other up. Susie got the feeling that Jack was just a looker. Jack noticed that Susie didn't have a wedding ring and had no family pictures on her desk or walls. Although Susie was seductive she was too old for Jack. She had divorced printed on her forehead. For Jack's real estate purpose, Susie would work out just fine.

The two flipped through a book of listings.

"I like that one," Jack said of a home in Palm Beach. The house was third from the top indicating that it was the third most expensive listing. The choice got Susie's attention. The house was her listing so she wouldn't have to split the broker's fee with another agency.

The pictures that Jack viewed showed a fully furnished home but upon arrival, the house was vacant. Susie turned off the burglar alarm, opened the door with her key and both entered.

Jack took a quick look around the vacant house and announced, "Nope, this one's not for me."

"No? Did you see the pool area?" Susie asked.

"Sorry. I just don't like it."

Jack thought, "Maybe I should just tell her that I want a fully furnished house with a large amount easily accessible cash and no dogs"

Jack realized that using a real estate broker was a bad idea. The cops would question the owner and the broker about who had viewed the place. Jack used Susie when he had stolen enough money to actually buy a house.

Plan B

Jack drove around looking for an appropriately sized house in a neighborhood that had space between the homes and was devoid of children's toys. Jack sought retirees and empty nesters. Kids, he felt, would suck up all of a family's disposable income.

Choosing a house to rob was much more difficult than he had anticipated. At first he sought homes that lacked security signs but realized that security systems were not a problem for him and the home security signs could be an indication that the residents had something to keep secure. Home security signs keep out amateur burglars. Jack, however, was a professional so he welcomed such signs.

Jack decided on the Palm Beach/West Palm Beach border. The houses were appropriately sized and the homes were not too close together.

He discovered a house at the end of a

short street. The house had no evidence of children. He could park at the end of the street for a stake out and could observe people who traveled the street. If someone saw him walking away after a robbery he figured that he would just give a neighborly wave.

Jack waited until 9:00 Pm on a Friday night in May. For the past two weeks the residents appeared not to be home Friday nights. The house across the street also seemed vacant on the target night and that was a bonus. Jack parked in the owner's driveway.

Nothing in the house would be taken that Friday night. The trial run was for observation and key making. The house was around 3,500 square feet and there was no evidence of children. Disabling the burglar alarm was simple and the small safe was in the entry way as expected. Jack made the front door key with the machine in his Jeep. Jack could make a key in around a minute. Jack could never understand why key makers in hardware stores took so long just to make a duplicate. He noted that the house was very nicely furnished with original art work.

Jack took a quick tour of the house while mentally recording every room, how many steps from the safe to the front and back doors. He opened the safe, observed $2,000.00 in cash, ten one ounce Kugerrands and jewelry.

Jack took nothing, reset the burglar alarm, and left. He timed himself taking a total of seventeen minutes to stake out the place. A slow drive down the street's slight incline showed nothing amiss in the sleepy neighborhood.

Jack returned the next Friday night and, as expected, the family was not home. The neighbors across the street appeared to be out also so Jack was ready for his first solo run.

The home had a two hundred foot concrete driveway with a convenient nook for Jack to be able to park inconspicuously.

Jack made his first mistake. He started to put on his black balaclava but decided not to wear it and left it between the front seats. He grabbed his duffel bag, donned his latex gloves, and proceeded to the front door.

Jack decided to use the front door for entry because the peep chains that people use would not be hitched if the occupants were away. If they were hitched the residents either were home or that they had exited from the garage. This house, conveniently, had no chain at all.

The entry way was beautiful with a sweeping "good morning" staircase. The chandelier, that every large home in Florida had in its entry, was prettier than most. Jack's tour of the downstairs revealed that no one was home and no dog was present. The den revealed a large TV, a very well stocked liquor cabinet and a disgusting ashtray with overflowing cigarette butts. The smell was overpowering. "If these people wanted to protect their valuables all that they need to do is put them in this room."

Jack opened the Thermidor refrigerator, took out a Corona, poured half down the sink and placed it on the breakfast nook table. He pulled one of the chairs out to make it look as if someone had sat there and drank half a beer.

The Corona trick would confuse the police. They would send it to the lab and it would reveal - absolutely nothing. No prints or saliva nor anything else. Such antics frustrated the investigators and used up their valuable time and resources.

Jack went straight to the safe. To Jack's pleasant surprise the safe held $4,000.00 and twelve one ounce gold Kugerrands. He quickly bagged everything, shut and locked the safe door, zipped the duffel bag, reset the alarm, and left with the loot.

That night Jack removed the key making machine and the duffel bag from the Jeep. The cash, coins and jewelry were placed in a shallow hole in his back yard that he had already dug.

Bright and early the next morning Jack took the coins and jewelry to Pickins, who would fence the non cash items. The black bag was put in the Jeeps rear compartment, out of sight. Just before he got to Pickins trailer, Jack was picked up on a radar trap. He was traveling at 47 mph on a 35 mph stretch of road. Jack thought about trying to make a get away but pulled over.

Jack lowered his window and kept his hands on the steering wheel. The Patrolman Paul

Webb, a Florida State Trooper, walked purposefully towards Jack.

"License and registration please."

Jack reached over to the glove compartment to retrieve his registration. It was then that Webb saw the black balaclava. Webb, who raced go-carts, knew exactly what the balaclava was (it is used under a racer's helmut as a fireproof measure).

"What's that?" questioned Webb pointing to the balaclava.

"My balaclava," answered Jack.

"What do you race?"

"Go-carts." drawing from his short very amateurish experience of driveway carting in Reading. It turned out to be a wrong answer.

"Where do you race?" Webb knew every go-cart track and cart racer in the state of Florida. Jack, however, wasn't among them.

Jack could see that the cop was getting suspicious and realized that he had to alter his story.

"I just goof off a bit in parking lots but I use a helmut and a balaclava."

"What kind of cart do you have?"

Jack paused since he was not familiar with go-cart manufacturers. "It has a 125 cc." His answer was incomplete and Webb thought it evasive. Real carters would have gone on with descriptions until the person had to be forced or begged to stop.

Webb smelled something suspicious with Jack's paused answer. He didn't know what but he suspected that something was not right. Webb was also aware that balaclavas were sometimes used by armed robbers of convenience stores and banks. Webb searched his brain for information on any recent hold ups where a balaclava was worn in a hold up but his search came up empty.

Please step out of the vehicle."

Jack knew not to protest and got out.

"May I see the balaclava?"

The fire resistant label on the inside of the balaclava indicated to Webb that it was for racing.

"Have you had anything to drink?"

"No. I don't drink."

"Ever?"

"Ever. And I don't smoke or take drugs."

Webb was impressed by Jack's answer surmising that Jack was probably a Born Again Christian and, in Webb's eyes, all Born Agains were fine people.

Webb was Born Again - as straight as an arrow. He had a great love of his family and love of The Lord. He assumed that Jack was similarly as Christian as he, possibly even more so, since Jack had never drank nor smoked.

Webb had messed up early in life but reformed himself. He had been truly born again. He credits his religious transformation with his reversal of his potential life of sin. Webb often told people that if he had not reformed he would have been put in jail instead of being someone who put others in jail. Webb shined his flashlight into Jack's eyes but saw nothing amiss.

Webb offered his hand to Jack, "I'm Paul."

"Jack."

"There's a race at Moroso on the 6th and attendance is free. Stop by."

Jack had turned around a possibly

disastrous situation into a new connection. Jack's luck was still with him.

Jack drove down the street, pulled over and threw up.

Jack's first burglary netted him just over $13,000.00. Despite the anxiety filled encounter with Webb, Jack knew that he was on to something big and the pickings were easy. He was eager to start his second break in.

Jack did not let the encounter with Webb go to waste. After setting out on a program to rob at least one house a week, he proceeded to buy a used go-cart and equipment for $2,000.00. Jack enjoyed buying a new helmut and a new racing suit.

The owner of Jack's new go-cart's son had been killed in an off road motor bike accident when the fourteen year old boy went off course and hit a tree. His neck snapped. The driver's mother just wanted to get rid of the cart.

"I'll sell you the hauler and parts for another thousand," said the grieving mother.

"Five hundred and you've got a deal."

"Sure. Take it away."

The two year old trailer, when new, cost $2,500.00 and it was filled with spare parts, rain and dry tires, a spare engine, spare seat, suspension parts, and tools.

Jack hauled his cart to Moroso for a regional event. He looked like a competitor with his brightly painted cart. His new helmut and suit gave him away as an amateur however. His helmut was plain white while most of the others had custom painted, wildly colored "hats". The seasoned drivers had nicer racing suits, with league and course patches, their names and blood types were embroidered on left chest area. Yes blood types. Cart racers have been known to end up paralyzed, dead or worse.

Jack practiced in the "Adult 125 class" - the drivers had to be over twenty years old and weigh over 125 pounds. The different classed were intended to literally separate the men from the boys. The boys were young hot shots with dreams of racing in NASCAR or Formula 1. Some of the men also harbored dreams of professional racing but really didn't have a snowball's chance. The Adult 125 class was competitive.

Jack started out embarrassingly slow in practice. Everyone had more experience than he did. He picked up some pointers from other drivers, got less timid with the right pedal, and used the left pedal less and less.

After practice, Trooper Webb came to Jack's trailer. "Jack, great to see you here."

Webb felt guilty for doubting Jack previously, so when Jack asked for advise, Webb was happy to help.

Webb produced a track map and guided Jack through every turn.

"There's no need to brake in turn 1. Off the gas, turn in, and just before the apex ease on the gas until you're full on the gas at the track out. Track out until you are almost on the grass and you won't spin but if you violate any of these suggestions you will either spin, or worse, you will be slow."

Webb went through each of the thirteen turns, showing Jack how to significantly decrease his lap times.

"Did I give you too much information?"

"No. I've got it."

Jack remembered and applied each and every piece of advise. Jack qualified tenth out of the fifteen drivers that would race in the fastest group.

In a LeMans start, the drivers stand across the track with their vehicles running. At the gun, the drivers sprint to their carts, jump in, and go. There are no seat belts to fasten. All fifteen drivers ran to their carts after the starting gun went off. Jack ran a little faster than some of the drivers that qualified ahead of him and picked up two positions. Jack applied the knowledge that Webb had imparted enabling him to pass two more drivers by the end of the first lap. Passing the slower drivers was much easier than passing the faster drivers. Each pass got harder and harder but Jack was braking later and softer and adding throttle earlier and harder.

With three laps to go Jack was in third place. Jack inched toward his next victim. He saw that the driver had a plain white helmut indicating that he was probably new to carting. The driver, however, was quite small and Jack knew that lightweight drivers had an advantage. Jack caught up to the slightly built driver but passing him would be much harder.

Going into turn one, Jack by barely lifted the gas pedal, was able to get just ahead of the guy. Moments before he went to full throttle the white helmeted driver turned into Jack's rear, swept him, and spun him out. Jack was enraged. Back hard on the gas, Jack didn't loose much time, and no one passed him.

Methodically Jack gained on his new enemy. He bumped the #3 cart in the back - bumping is a signal to the lead driver that the back car can and will pass. On occasion the lead driver will give the back driver some room to pass. The front driver did not. Jack then proceeded to sweep the #3 cart, spinning him out.

Jack was tired and his tires too hot to lap as fast as he had been lapping. The #3 cart again caught up to him and tried to initiate another sweep but Jack avoided it by going wide into turn 5. Going wide enabled the #3 cart to pass him.

Jack finished third, cart #3 finished second, and Paul Webb finished first. Jack was still livid and sought the driver of #3 for a confrontation. The #3's driver had just parked the cart and stood up when Jack arrived. The driver of #3 was just removing his helmut when Jack realized that the driver was a woman. A long browned haired, drop dead beautiful woman. She removed her helmut and shook her thick long brown hair just like a model in a shampoo commercial. Jack was awe struck by the woman's beauty.

She was not Jack's type. She looked her age - twenty-six (Jack liked women who looked or were sixteen), her weight was average (Jack liked very slim women) but she was beautiful and had an absolute killer smile.

She smiled that killer smile at Jack, extending her right hand, "Natalie."

"Jack."

"I see that you two have met," Webb said jokingly as he approached his wife and Jack.

Jack generally slept very little; usually only four hours each night. The night after the race, after having met Natalie, he couldn't sleep at all. The picture of Natalie removing her helmut, with her gorgeous hair cascading to her shoulders played over and over. Her charm and smile haunted his sleep. Jack wanted Natalie in a way he had never wanted any woman previously. Jack was smitten and for the first time in his life the attraction wasn't simply sexual.

Jack and Webb practiced with their carts every Tuesday during open track nights at Moroso. Jack perfected his racing techniques compulsively just like everything he engaged in.

"Keep your eyes up. Don't just look at the cart in front of you, look ahead and into the corner's exit," Webb instructed.

Jack learned the technique of using the gas and brake at the same time.

"If you keep the right pedal to the floor while you brake you won't loose as much engine speed. Your front tires won't grip as much because there won't be as much weight on the front but you'll learn to adjust," Webb taught him.

Webb taught Jack to not brake before tight corners but rather to enter the turn at full throttle and then brake just after entering the turn - a technique referred to as trail braking. Jack really liked trail braking not only because it was faster but also because of its risk factor.

"If you're not scared, you're not going fast enough," Webb advised.

Jack and Webb became good friends.

Jack paid for their two carts to be hauled to Connecticut, paid for two Interlaken Hotel rooms, food, and first class airfare.

Neither man had ever flown first class before, in fact Jack had never been in an airplane. Webb paid for the rental car but did so with the understanding that only Jack would drive.

By the time the two left Florida, in mid summer, Jack was flush with cash. Jack's Florida burglaries had netted him around $200,000.00. Jack was able to rob homes with ease while the homes occupants were spending their summers in the cooler climates around

Maine's coast, the Hamptons, Cape Cod, and New Hampshire's Lake Winnipesaukee. Jack was extremely disappointed when Natalie declined to accompany the guys on the trip to Lime Rock but Natalie wasn't feeling well.

Jack loved and hated his first airplane ride. Flying itself was a magical feat. How could something the size and weight of the massive plane get up in the air Jack wondered. There was a majesty in flying. Jack, however, was not the plane's pilot and he was not in control which scared the shit out of him. He vowed to learn how to fly and he did.

The Lime Rock race was a regional event but a very competitive one. Extremely wealthy racers from New York, Massachusetts and Connecticut raced. Many of the drivers were A plus personalities who were used to winning at everything they did. Jack quickly discovered that many of the competitors had homes in southern Florida. He got the addresses of the Florida homes from the race registry thus giving him a menu of potential new victims.

Ninety-three racers participated in the

Lime Rock event. Racers were randomly divided into three groups and given twenty laps for practice. Drivers were then separated into one of the three groups, according to their practice speed.

After the practice session, each group had ten laps to qualify for the start. Jack qualified second and Webb qualified for P1. If a driver didn't get into the fastest group he or she had no chance of winning the top prize. Top prize was a somewhat larger trophy. No money, just glory.

Jack and Webb "walked the track" with most of the other racers. Webb and Jack listened intently to the race instructors and Webb showed Jack additional tricks to help eek out as much speed as possible. Since all the carts were "spec" none of them should have had an technical advantage. The race was to be won by the driver with the most skill and balls.

It should not come as a surprise but racers have been known to cheat. Three carts were disqualified after inspection. One of the guys was eliminated for having lightened his cart then added weight from lead from X-ray aprons. The lead was Sandwiched between a double flooring. The lead weight lowered the cart's center of gravity making it more stable.

Jack's conversation with the lead apron cheat revealed that Rob was a bond and penny stock brokerage owner with 150 employees. Jack actually didn't understand what Rob's business did but he liked that it was, as Rob put it, an "edgy" business.

Rob owned a twenty room home in Connecticu. Because of all the horse stables on the property, town zoning would not allow him to build a twenty-four car garage, so Rob had a thirty-two car garage built underground. The garage had an elevator, gasoline pumps, two car lifts, massive tool boxes, a full time mechanic and its own car wash.

Jack got excited when Rob mentioned that he had a winter home. Unfortunately the winter home was in Costa Rica, not Florida. Jack didn't even know where Costa Rica was.

Rob was an advocate for weight equalized carts. Even if he had not been eliminated for attempting to cheat, Rob's 265 pounds would have made an overall win virtually impossible. Even though Rob was only forty-two years old, he was ready for the grave. His bad habits had bad habits. Upon waking Rob would manage to drink a black coffee before his first beer. Rob's driver, Enrique, would usually have to wait until after Rob's second beer to chauffeur Rob to the office in New York City.

"No bumps Enrique."

Enrique had to make sure that Rob's first cocaine of the day would not spill. Enrique was very willing to overlook Rob's shortcomings since his $100,000.00 salary, plus bonuses, was more money than he ever dreamed of making.

Rob drank heavily, used drugs regularly, weighed way more than he should, loved strip clubs and massage parlors, and stretched the Securities and Exchange Commission's laws way beyond their limits.

Rob asked Jack to meet him for breakfast on Sunday morning after the race.

"Should I bring Webb with me?"

"No, no, no. I like Webb but not the cop part."

"We pump and dump penny stocks," explained Rob.

Jack gave Rob a puzzled look.

"Penny stocks are stocks of companies that sell for less than a dollar a share. They're stocks of companies that are on the ropes or have a nine count. We cold call widows and orphans and appeal to their greed.

"You can buy 5,000 shares of Mercury Process Mining for $1,000.00 - a mere 20 cents a share. We expect MPM to go to $2.00 in the next month and $4.00 in six months. You could be sitting on twenty grand for a mere $1,000.00 investment. If you can afford to buy 50,000 shares your financial worries will be over."

"Sounds like a good deal."

"Don't be stupid. I already bought a million shares for a penny a piece. The EPA has closed the company down. Mercury is not a healthy element for people. Not only is MPM toast, there is nowhere to sell the stock. I'll make ten million and my brokers will split the other ten million in commissions. We do one of these every ten days."

Jack was intrigued.

"If you're interested in selling for me, you can easily make a million your first year. My top guys make five."

"I'll give it some thought. I was also wondering if you would ever be interested in high quality jewelry and one ounce Suisse gold? Twenty ounces at a wack."

"Definitely," Rob winked.

In less than one year Rob was indicted on all sorts of charges, his penny stock company was closed by the SEC, and the widows and orphans were using their stock certificates as toilet paper.

Enrique started his own limousine business and sold a little cocaine on the side. All 150 of Rob's salespeople were living in their mother's guest rooms or were in rehab. None of Rob's staff ever saved a dime, since their salaries went right back to Rob who supplied them with cocaine.

Rob sold thirty of his thirty-two cars. He lost money on all the cars except his three Ferraris. Since Rob needed a large cash flow to support his life style and lawyers, he was glad to help Jack with his excess jewelry inventory. Jack ceased to be jewelry adverse since Rob paid him twice as much as Pickins did.

The Lime Rock race began.

In racing, a flying start is where all the drivers must remain in their qualifying positions, as they drive slowly towards the green flag, can be messy. When the green flag was waived, the cart in P3, behind Webb, had accelerated prematurely. P3 ran into P1 Webb, spinning out both drivers. Webb managed to reenter the race in thirteenth position. The race was only forty-five minutes long, so Webb had a great deal of catching up to do. Jack took over the lead.

Webb raced his heart out. Early passes were easy but as he advanced, catching and overtaking became more and more difficult since drivers toward the front of the pack had increasingly faster lap times. Webb finally was in second place with three laps to go. He caught up to Jack and was able to bump him.

Turn one was marked by a "turn in cone" like the cones used on road construction sites. The cone was there as a suggested turn-in point, not a mandatory marker.

On the second to last lap Jack was convinced that Webb would pass him in turn one, which was at the end of the longest straight, and the best place for passing. Jack and Webb went as fast as they could towards turn one, only to come upon a slow cart which both drivers would have to pass.

The slow driver took the left turn by going around outside of the cone. At the very last possible moment, Jack turned left inside the cone (a legal maneuver) enabling him to pass the slower cart without significantly slowing. Webb was obliged to pass the slow cart on the outside costing him time and first place.

Jack took the checkered flag and did his parade lap. He was in heaven. At the finish, Webb and Jack hugged like two old army buddies. Webb was proud of his student and Jack proud of his first win.

Jack visited the Webb's home frequently.

The two men worked on their go-carts and talked about life. Jack would often bring steaks and potato salad for Natalie, Paul and himself.

Jack loved to look at and talk to Natalie. Jack loved Natalie's smile and subtly flirtatious manner.

Webb never had any indication of Jack's criminal escapades. Only once did Webb ask Jack what he did for a living. Jack's reply was, "investments." Both men left it at that. Webb assumed that Jack had inherited wealth because Boston had wealthy people from old money and families.

Webb and Jack where working on Jack's cart which was on a stand. Jack noticed that Webb still had on his regulation shoes.

"Why don't you guys wear sneakers?" asked Jack.

"Regulations. But next month we are getting black leather sneakers designed and made by Nike. We're supposed to get baseball caps soon too, so that we don't have to wear the ugly regulation ones that we currently have."

Such information was valuable to Jack.

The old police shoes were not an asset for cops on a foot chase. Jack appreciated knowing that if he ever had to run from the police he could no longer count on having a footwear advantage.

A month later Webb showed Jack his new Nike regulation footwear.

"Those old ones sucked," Jack commented.

"Yep. New shoes and a new job next week. I'm being promoted to detective."

A cold chill enveloped Jack. "Are you going to investigate all those burglaries?"

"No, that's local cops. I'll be investigating drug crimes."

Webb knew that Jack was interested in the Florida burglaries so he innocently told Jack anything he learned. Most of what Webb offered, Jack already knew. Occasionally Webb's feedback was really helpful.

"One guy at headquarters found a pattern in the burglaries. The guy thinks that the Shore Road area will get hit next Friday night."

Jack had actually planned a robbery two

streets north of Shore Road for Friday night. Jack hadn't even realized that his burglaries had a pattern to them. He would modify his break-in patterns.

Friday night Jack drove around the Shore Road area just to observe. Sure enough, there were unmarked police vehicles parked and cruising. Jack noted that every one of the undercover four door sedans had small "moon cap" hubcaps and black-wall tires. He made note of and remembered every make, model, and year of the unmarked cop cars. Without Webb's inadvertent tip he would most likely been caught.

Webb and Jack often worked on their carts together at Webb's house. Natalie often brought the men iced tea or lemonade on a tray. She brought the guys home made cookies and always included a napkin for each man. Sometimes there was even a flower in a vase - it showed that she cared.

Natalie had not eaten with the two men the last two times Jack brought dinner. Natalie had not been looking well the last time Jack saw her. Natalie had lost weight which made her face look gaunt. Her new short hair had lost its luster and waviness. Her normally red smiling lips were colorless and devoid of lust. She looked fifteen years older. Jack wondered if she was sick or depressed.

On the most recent visit to the Webbs, Natalie spent the evening in bed and didn't even go outside to talk to the boys. Jack missed the lemon aid, the cookies, and even the flowers, but most of all he missed Natalie.

"What's wrong with her Paul?" Jack wondered.

"I don't know Jack. I don't know."

"Well what's the doctor say?"

"I haven't taken her to the doctor. We've been praying a lot though."

Jack screamed, "You've been praying! Praying when your wife can't even get out of bed? Are you stupid?"

"You've got to leave Jack. Get off my property."

Jack threw his fork to the table and walked off. Jack never returned to the Webb house. He simply left his go-cart, trailer, and tools. He never raced or even sat in a go-cart again and he never again talked to Webb.

Webb knew that Jack was right. He felt stupid for not bringing Natalie to the doctor sooner. That night, Webb's doctor told Webb to bring Natalie directly to the hospital.

Stage IV Pancreatic cancer was the diagnosis. The cancer had spread to Natalie's lymph nodes. She was given three months to live.

Natalie would be dead in a month.

A GOOD HIT

Jack enjoyed the thrill of staking the houses that he wanted to burglarize.

The wealthiest victims, who would be robbed, were approached with greater caution than the mere rich. Wealthy neighborhoods were much more often patrolled by police or private security. A simple stake out was too risky. Jack would go to the robbery victim's home with a rake, shovel, and some red stones and start to work on the house's landscaping. If the owner came home, Jack would feign that he went to the wrong address and would even produce even a work order showing a discrepant address.

"Can you pay me for the work I've done?" he would ask his victims if he was confronted. Jack rarely got caught doing his landscaping/stalking work but if he did he was covered. If Jack was discovered, about half the time, the homeowner would pay him something for his labor.

Several people not only paid Jack for his work but even asked him for a business card. Jack scratched a fake phone number on his fake work order. He left the company name and address knowing that it could not be traced to him. Jack had lifted work order forms from the desk of the company where he bought the red stones.

If the homeowner confronted Jack while he was doing his alleged landscaping, Jack would not rob the home. He realized that he could be identified so he went on to other homes. There were plenty of other homes to choose from of course.

By doing pseudo landscaping Jack would figure out what kind of security system the owner had. Jack would also look for any evidence of a dog. Big protection dogs would dissuade Jack. Yappy dogs could be quickly addressed with pepper spray or a stun gun. Big dogs simply weren't worth the effort. Jack would move on, sometimes to the house next door.

Jack started robbing houses similar of size to those that he knew from growing up in Reading. He robbed middle class comfortable homes. After fencing his stolen goods his "earnings" amounted to an unimpressive ten cents on the dollar for jewelry, 50% for gold but cash was 100% his. Jack realized that the effort necessary to rob moderately large homes and risk involved, was not enough to justify the proceeds.

Jack had two options: he could sell the stolen goods himself or rob homes with greater valuables or some combination of the two. Jack carefully (Jack was careful) increased the size of the burgled homes thus increasing the size of his take. Southern Florida, fortunately for Jack, had an abundance of mansion size homes to choose from.

Jack's carnival lifestyle allowed him a wide area to rob. Jack continued to run his carnival game even after he had purchased a house in Florida. Jack enjoyed being the "King Carny" who had money to burn.

One major problem with homes that had a large quantity of valuables was that they were most often protected with increasingly more sophisticated burglar alarms and many had larger, harder to open, safes. Some safes, particularly older models, are fairly easy to break open. Since one of his fences was a locksmith, Jack was able to learn more sophisticated locksmithing techniques. Being able to disable burglar alarms and to open most locked safes enabled him to rob almost any size home. Jack actually found that many safes were never locked because the owners were too lazy to close and reopen them. Bypassing even the most sophisticated burglar alarms was a technique that was not too difficult for Jack to master.

Jim and Jill's house was, for Jack, conveniently located on a canal. Accessing the house by boat was far less obvious than access by car.

The house was on a peninsula between a canal and the Inland waterway. Jack sped along the coast's open water until he got to a waterway entrance, and then slowly motored into the canal where the homes boat was docked.

Jack's center console inflatable with its 75 horsepower Mercury motor was fast. The dark grey boat with black motor was hard to see at night if the running lights were off. Jack tied up the inflatable to the stern of Bill's sixty-five foot Pacemaker motor yacht with the inflatable's bow out. The Mercury motor was left running while Jack went ashore.

It took Jack a mere twenty minutes to disable the security system, find and open the safe and escape with the family's valuables. Jack didn't take anything heavy and did no property damage. Cash and easily fence-able valuables are all a professional thief wants.

Jack knew that most of the goods he had taken would be recoverable by the homeowner's insurance. If he had done damage or taken cherished items, then the homeowner would seek vengeance. A vengeful victim can be a bigger threat than the police.

Jack threw his bag of goods into the inflatable and jumped on board. He quietly motored out of the connecting canal and turned on the craft's running lights as he entered the Inland Waterway.

Jack's thefts afforded him a house in Florida, another in Maine, a 40' speedboat, two planes and had his own helicopter.

BOCA BURGLARY #222

Jennie and Jim lived in a 6,425 square foot house in Boca Raton Florida. The seven bedroom, seven bathroom house is situated on two acres. The house, with traditional stucco exterior and red tile roof was in immaculate condition and the property was landscaped to perfection. The house was situated on a canal just off the Inland Waterway. There was a wall of windows that overlooked the pool, a maze of decks, a barbecue pit and wonderful flower gardens. Beyond the pool fence there was a spectacular view of the Inland Waterway, a parade of yachts, and palm trees.

Since he was not a billionaire Bill was not listed as one of Forbes Magazine's 400 wealthiest people in America. By most every other standard Bill had done very well financially.

Bill was never a good student since he had learning issues and has always had problems with test taking. He graduated from a middle level college in his home state of Ohio. He graduated 295th out of 305 students but he did graduate with a bachelor's degree in accounting.

Bill's fraternity brothers helped him graduate. He was tutored, he was in study groups, and was encouraged by his fraternity brothers in every possible way. All of Bill's fraternity brothers knew that Bill would receive $50,000.00 from his grandfather upon graduation. But, he had to graduate. Bill was a tight end on the Mid Ohio College football team. Since football was everything at Mid Ohio and Bill was an essential part of the team. The fraternity brothers gave Bill their all but knew that he had to graduate.

Tall, handsome, likable, and smart; Bill could simply not take tests well. He would panic and sweat. Anxiety overwhelmed him so that his hands would shake at the start of each test. As he progressed through the test, his symptoms got worse, knowing that he was screwing it up.

On one Western Civilization final, the instructions were to answer one of three questions. Bill answered all three, two were answered poorly and one was well done but by answering all three, Bill ran out of time, so he failed the test.

Bill's frat brothers offered a variety of ideas that they though might help:

"Bill. Try a little ganja before the next test."

It didn't work.

"Bill. Take a Valium before the next test."

That didn't work either.

"Bill. Take a shot of Jack before the test."

Chemicals simply didn't help Bill's testing problems.

Somehow Bill managed to graduate. As Bill stepped from the podium, after getting his diploma and shaking appropriate hands, Bill's grandfather (also named Bill) greeted him with a massive bear hug. The colorful grandfather carried a custom made leather satchel with Bill's fraternity letters silk screened on two sides..

"I love my bag Grandpa."

"Open it."

The bag contained 500 one hundred dollar bills. Bill's grandfather was an Ohio wildcat oil well driller who had never even graduated from high school. The grandfather went to college vicariously through his grandson. As soon as Bill got his diploma and walked down the podium his proud grandfather met him. The two men hugged each other and cried.

"You know that I would have given you

that money even if you didn't graduate."

"I probably did know but it gave me the incentive to go on when I needed a push. Thank you for your support."

"I'm so proud of you Bill."

"And I'm proud of you too Bill."

The day after graduation, Bill and his fraternity brother Brian, sat at a secluded restaurant table.

"I've got an idea for a restaurant."

The concept was for a restaurant chain for youthful sports enthusiasts. The restaurants would be a place where college age and post college age people could go and watch sports, drink, and eat barbecued chicken. The restaurants would be for entertainment as much as eating.

"I think that if the first restaurant takes that we could have hundreds across America,"

Brian proceeded, "If you invest $10,000.00 you will get 1 million shares of 'Brest 'n Legs' stock at a penny a share."

Bill knew that Brian was a "player" and went along with the extremely long shot venture. "Brest 'n Legs" eventually had 1100 locations in six countries and the publicly traded stock is worth just under $200.00 - per share. Bill did just fine for a guy who couldn't take a test.

BILL'S HOUSE #322

Jack and his girlfriend had gone shopping for an engagement ring three weeks before Thanksgiving. The south east coast of Florida is awash in jewelry stores. Just when Jack's girlfriend was about to make a decision one of the pair would pick out some flaw. "Its too big or I really want a yellow diamond or wouldn't white gold be pretty?" they said as a stall.

They delayed long enough to observe a well dressed mature woman who became a mark. The woman's black hair was perfect with slight reddish hue. She wore a fairly short black skirt with a tight fitting rose colored knit top. Jennie looked great for her age. She was a typical southern Florida woman who kept fit and could afford the best care to keep her looks up. Jack saw that the woman was buying a $7,500.00 Breitling Bentley watch, which Jack overheard, was for her husband for Christmas.

"His Rolex is now simply too difficult for him to read. I guess he's just getting old. I might have to trade HIM in for a new one," she joked.

When the woman was about to pay Jack and his girlfriend hastily excused themselves and proceeded to their car. Jack followed Jennie home.

January 1, 1975 Bill's wife Jennie awoke after a hairy New Years eve party. She was not in top shape having returned home after 2:00 AM and having consumed her share of champagne. Jennie laid in bed with a snow white comforter covering her tanned body. She looked good for a middle aged woman who had two sons and one granddaughter.

Jennie placed her jewelry on her night stand before collapsing on her bed around 2:15 AM. The only things that she needed to accomplish that morning were to hang up her skimpy black dress, which she had left in a pile on the floor, and put her jewelry in the jewelry box and into the safe. She awoke around 8:00 AM and hoped that a hot shower would bring some life back to her tired body.

Even before the New Years eve party she was worn out. She and Jim had been in Maine for Thanksgiving through Christmas visiting their son and their new granddaughter. The trip and festivities had taken a toll on Jill.

"Jim, have you seen my jewelry box?"

"No, but it might be in the safe."

"Will you open the safe for me please?"

"As soon as I get back from the drugstore honey."

"Please pick up some Advil dear. And can you pick up Moses at the kennel?"

"We can get Moses tomorrow."

"But I miss the old hound."

"How about this afternoon?"

"I love you."

After coffee and then a bloody Mary, Jennie laid down for a short nap. Jim returned (no, he didn't forget the Advil) and, as promised, opened the safe.

"What the hell?" Jim Yelled.

"What's the matter honey?"

"I think that we've been robbed."

"What do you mean, robbed?"

"Our money and jewelry are gone."

Indeed the couple had been robbed. Jim always kept exactly $25,000.00 in cash in the safe - bail money he used to call it. Also missing was around $80,000.00 in gold coins and small gold bars, Jennie's jewelry box had been looted of everything solid gold and all the quality gem jewelry was gone. The few sterling silver pieces were left as were a few low quality gems. The jewelry was worth $150,000.00. Stock certificates were left but the $100,000.00 in bearer bonds were gone. Jim's brand new Breitling Bentley and Rolex Mariner watches were gone too.

Detectives Maloney and Gonzales responded. "This looks like a very professional job," Maloney stated.

"What do you mean "professional job"? asked Jim.

"Nothing other than the safe was touched.

Nothing in the house was broken and nothing like TVs or stereos were taken. Amateurs take hard to carry TVs and stupid things because they can; they just go wild. They go through dresser drawers and throw socks on the floor. For some reason they always smash lamps. Last year some punks even stole a guy's condoms. Pros take cash, gold, jewelry, and easy to carry items that can easily be fenced," Mahoney stated.

Gonzales knew a bit about jewelry. "They didn't even take the sterling or semi precious stones."

"The good thing about professionals is that they rarely return."

"Can you give us a list of what was taken? Also please, a list of who might have done work on the inside or outside of your house in the last year."

"I just gave Jim that Breitling watch for Christmas," Jennie added.

"I never even wore it."

"I'm sorry honey."

"Since I didn't have it long enough to get fond of it we can get another."

"You're so sweet. Come back to bed."

The list of missing valuables and contractors were supplied to the detectives but the case was never solved. Insurance paid for most of the losses.

Jack pocketed the $25,000.00 in cash. He fenced the $80,000.00 in gold coins at half the value. The bearer bonds and the gold jewelry was harder to fence so he only got 10% of the value. A net take of $130,000.00 for three weeks work was not bad. The brand new Breitling Bentley watch fit Jack's wrist just perfectly while the Rolex was given to the fence as a tip. In the 1970s, $130,000.00 was what a surgeon would earn in a year.

BIGGER HAULS #649

While staking out another house in Palm Beach Jack realized that several houses in the neighborhood had no one at home. Also, the house adjacent to the canal could be used as an access point for two non canal homes across the street. He could hit two or three homes at the same time.

Holidays were favorites for Jack. Either rich people would be home having big parties or they would be at other people's houses having a party during holidays. They would drink too much and in many who Jack burglarized, didn't even realize that they had been robbed for days after.

Jack's fake groundskeeper technique kept working like a charm. Families who would be having big parties generally prepared for them for days in advance. Yards were made immaculate by real groundskeepers. Pools were cleaned and brought to the correct Ph. level. Food and drinks were brought in by the van load. There was a high level of preparation and therefore evidence that they would be home or not. The 4th of July was only three weeks away which gave Jack just enough time to plan his first multi home break in. He was excited, enervated and already counting his chickens.

Jack would always keep to his rules: Never take personal items - except jewelry, never take anything heavy, never break anything, or destroy property. Whenever possible, access the property by water and if someone appears just leave fast. Run like hell.

Two of the three homes were a piece of cake. All three homes were built by the same builder, all three had the same security systems, and all three had their safes in about the same spot. All three home's occupants had gone to the same party. The owners of the three houses were picked up in the same stretch limousine which insured that they would return at the same time. Jack even though of sending a free limousine to pick up his next victims.

Ironically someone had thought of that limo idea around the same time. The burglar gave his victims free sports tickets and a free limousine ride. Unfortunately for the burglar, his technique was reported in the newspaper and the next recipient of free tickets reported the gift to the police. The burglar was caught. Adding insult to injury, the group whose homes were to get broken into actually went in the limo and attended the baseball game while the police arrested the burglars.

Jack had his system down pat. He had a landscaping truck nicely lettered with a telephone number that went to an answering service. Jack had business cards and he had printed work orders. He was welcomed into gated communities as a landscaper by the guards, who almost never asked questions.

If victims were asked to report workers who had preformed services on their property, Jack's name would not be listed because he was never actually hired to do work. The answering service actually got calls from families requesting Jack's services.

There were many particulars about the Dade and Broward County robberies that confused the Florida police. Jack intentionally did confusing things, like his half empty Corona trick. Jack did not fit the profile of a typical burglar either. Most burglars would have stopped after accumulating large sums of money, or stopped and restarted after they snorted, shot up, or gambled away the funds. Not Jack. Jack was a prolific predator who was really not in control of his compulsions.

Jack needed to be the #1 burglar in America. Jack also needed the thrill of the chase.

At some point Jack probably became a suspect in the Florida burglaries but, as with his go-cart exploits in Reading, he had to be caught driving in the street.

Since Jack was not a substance abuser he couldn't be ratted on by an arrested drug dealer who was trying to get a beak. Jack's drug was the thrill of the stalking, the thrill of breaking in, and the thrill of outsmarting the police.

Jack got away with his burglaries for fifteen years. Jack had his system down pat. Cash is untraceable. Gold was melted down within a day by his fence. The fence sold any really valuable coins, jewelry and all gems in Europe. The expensive jewelry would be worn by women who flew to Ireland and Holland to help fence it.

The estimate of Jack's thefts, $133,000,000.00 is a lot of money and it was the result of a lot of burglaries. Jack was a tireless worker who labored 365 days a year at his profession. The sheer number of burglaries and the wide area of his thefts overwhelmed the police.

Jack pulled up to the marina's gas dock and filled the inflatable's gas tanks. The dock boy cleated the boat's lines and threw the lines to Jack after the tanks were full. Jack paid for the fifty gallons of gas with cash and gave the dock boy a twenty dollar tip. Jack had already made trips three times that week. Once during the day and twice at night. He used a hand held navigation unit just in case a mounted unit could be traced. If he got stopped the hand held unit would be dropped overboard.

Jack loved being out on the water in his inflatable. He was not restricted to roads and gates, the wind was cool, and the salt spray was refreshing.

It took twenty-two minutes to get to his destination arriving just before nightfall. Since the fireworks would start at dark and he wanted to approach the houses dust after dark, he actually had a fairly narrow window to do his work.

July 3 was a hot night without a cloud in the sky and only a sliver of a moon. Being out on the water was really pleasant. He kept the boat at 4 mph which is the speed limit for the Inland Waterway. The target house was the first one on a canal just off the waterway.

As he always did, Jack reversed the inflatable so that it was to the stern of the owner's vessel with the inflatable's bow out, ready to go. The incoming tide held the inflatable's port side tight to the "CHILDS PLAY"- a 40' Post equipped for sport fishing. Jack cleated his lines to the vessel. Jack appreciated the boat's name since it was owned by Fred Childs.

Gaining entry to Childs' house was not difficult for Jack. He walked across the lawn and hopped over the four foot chain link fence into the pool area. A chain link fence was used by the Childs because it didn't block the view from the house to the canal. Direct view of the canal from the house would give Jack a heads up in case any marine patrol vessels approached. Jack appreciated how nice the yard was and its landscaping. Six cushioned chaise lounges were set up with near perfect spacing between them. There was a maze of teak decks with teak handrails. The sixteen foot long by six feet tall stone barbecue pit, made of fieldstone, had a six propane burners. The house had a wall of glass overlooking the pool area.

Jack quickly disabled the ten year old security system and, with his pre maid keys, unlocked the two locks on the back door of the house. Once inside, he went through the house quickly to insure that no one was home, went to the safe and opened it. There was a stack of $100 bills about two inches thick. Jack knew that it totaled around $10,000.00. There was a canvas bag of collector gold coins and twenty-five one ounce Suisse gold bars worth about $1,500.00 each. There was about two and a half pounds of jewelry which Jack did not take the time to sort through. Everything went into his black canvas bag and he was quickly out the front door.

After finishing at the Childs' house, Jack went across the street to the next house's front door. The alarm system was the same make and age as the Childs'. Timing himself, he was able to disable it fifteen seconds faster than the one that he disabled minutes earlier. Everything for Jack was a contest. He had made a key for the two front door locks earlier, so access was fast. The safe was a bit of a puzzle for Jack as it was quite large for a residence and it was fairly new. Cracking the safe took more time than he liked. He had never cracked that particular model before.

Jack stood in awe after opening the safe door. There were four one foot stacks of $100 bills. A quick calculation indicated $250,000.00 in cash. Jack threw the jewelry from the first house into the safe to make room for the cash which he crammed into his duffel bag.

He made a hasty retreat out the front door, checked for traffic and dog walkers and sprinted across the street. Once across the street he stopped, took a breath and calmed himself down. Now was not a good time to make a mistake. He removed his balaclava and walked briskly to the inflatable.

The third house was spared since Jack didn't have any more room in his bag. He considered dumping the cash into his bait box and returning to the third house but decided against it.

The boat's motor started on first try, Jack uncleated his bow and stern lines and slowly motored into the Inland Waterway. Once he turned his running lights on he felt some relief. It was his biggest cash haul ever. Just as he was pulling into the canal Jack saw the limousine arrive at the houses.

Jack really liked Herreshoff* cleats. Most people think that Nathaniel (Nat) Herreshoff designed the cleats for his America's Cup boat but Jack knew that they were really designed so that pirates like he could make a quick getaway after robbing nice houses.

Jack realized that the large amount of cash from the second house was probably acquired in some illegal way. Normal people simply do not keep that much cash around. The loss would probably not be reported to the police or the owner's insurance company. He wondered how the second home owner would deal with the jewelry found in the safe. The haul was around $300,000.00. Enough to buy the house in Vinalhaven Maine that he wanted.

*Captain Natanael Herreshoff, born March 18, 1848, was an incredible naval architect. Herreshoff designed yachts won five America's Cup races. Captain Nat skippered his first America's Cup yacht, the Vigilant. to victory in the 1893 America's Cup race. He designed and built the world's first torpedo boat and the first catamaran. He invented the sail track and slide which is still used.

The Herreshoff cleat is still used to secure the lines on all types vessel. The Herrashoff Cleat is a "T" with two legs. Wrapping a vessels lines to the cleat properly secures the lines yet allows fast removal.

BIG BUSINESS #1333

Just like any good business person Jack realized that he had to increase volume in order to increase profits. Increasing the margins on his products was not an option since cash is cash, melting gold into bars himself seemed like too much work and too much exposure and he didn't have enough knowledge of gems or the connections to get to the next level of fencing. Robbing bigger homes did not substantially increase his net take because most people only kept a limited amount of cash and gold at home. There was more jewelry in larger residences but the net take on jewelry was really marginal since it had to be fenced. Hitting multiple homes in the same neighborhood had doubled his take but still he wanted more.

Jack decided to try a one entry burglary scenario. Not staking out homes for weeks and not reentering to make keys or memorize the floor plan would enable him to rob many more homes. Less time casing the victim's residences also meant that fewer people could observe his actions. There was downside risk however. Not having premade keys would necessitate picking entry locks thus taking more time during the actual robbery. If he were to get caught in the initial entry he would face unlawful entry charges only but he would probably get linked to his other burglaries. One hit burglaries certainly carried more risk. Burglary with unlawful entry was a much more serious offense.

Jack's tried a new technique for close observation that would allow him to approach the house and even looking in the windows to be considered an acceptable behavior. He changed the van from being a landscaping business to a flower delivery business. He would hold flowers in his hand and leave one or two bouquets in the van. His girlfriend and his neighbors got a lot of his left over flowers.

A knock on the victim's door would generally reveal a dog's presence. He might even be able to take a look around back. Twice when residents were home he ended up giving them bouquets.

Jack had magnetic signs made for the sides of his Jeep. Jack-Be-Nimble Flowers was the best that he could think of for a name. He also could easily convert to his old standby of being a landscaper by quickly switching the magnetic signs.

Jack knew exactly which house he wanted

to rob first using his new one stop technique. It was a house that he had longed to see inside. The entrance to the driveway was from a four foot thick stone wall and had a gate with one and a quarter inch thick iron bars. The stone wall had a copper and glass lantern atop each pillar. The solid brass sign said WINDY HILL even though there was no hill. The circular driveway led to the stone house. Two huge flowers pots stood at each side of the house's entrance. To the left appeared to be a four car garage but it was actually two cars deep. The roof was slate not red tile like the roof on most Florida homes. Three chimneys protruded high past the roofline.

He knocked on the front door and rang the door bell. Apparently no one was home and he heard no barking. He walked around to the burglar alarm and quickly disabled it. Back to the van for lock picking tools. The front door locks were easy for Jack. The home's security system was not state of the art. Luckily there were no staff people or grounds keepers present that day.

Each stone on the facade of the house had

a code number on the bottom, written in white grease pencil. The whole house had been dismantled in Winchester Massachusetts and reassembled in Palm Beach. Each stone had been removed, categorized, cleaned, and palletized before being shipped to Florida by barge for reassembly. The owner wanted a slate roof, not Spanish tile, so each piece of slate was removed and shipped. The home's post and beam frame was likewise dismantled and reassembled. The task was monumental in time and cost. The original house had 6,000 square feet of floor space and a 4,000 square foot addition was added in Florida. The completed house had eleven bathrooms, seven bedrooms, three living rooms, two dining rooms and three kitchens. One of the kitchens was solely for entertaining guests during pool parties. Jack thought that the gift wrapping room was way too much.

Jack was surprised that the outdoor pool was smallish. The indoor pool was also small as it was the kind that flows water so that the swimmer doesn't have to turn around - a swim spa and they weren't supposed to be big. There were metal lockers like the ones from high school in the pool's shower room. Jack wondered why some of the lockers were padlocked.

The two walk in closets were larger than most people's bedrooms. Jack especially loved the men's cigar and wine tasting room. All four walls were lined with wine bottles. Eight comfortable arm chairs surrounded a mahogany table which sat atop a thick oriental rug. A desk size humidor held a large selection of cigars including illegal Cubans. Jack was tempted to take a few Cubans but knew that kind of shit gets guys busted. Jack would never smoke the cigars but certain friends would love to smoke them.

The main living room had a six foot wide fireplace across from which was a large oil portrait of some female ancestor who was dressed in fancy clothes. Under one window was a three foot wide by thirty inch tall wooden sculpture of a cowboy riding a horse. A small brass plaque showed the sculptor to be Fredrick

Remington. Jack liked the sculpture so much he considered stealing it.

There was no safe to be found so he went to the bedroom only to find a minimal amount of jewelry. He ran through the house until he found a home office. There was a desk whose drawers revealed nothing of value. To his back was a cabinet with a key in the lock.

"These people are way too careless," he thought.

Sure enough, the cabinet contained $20,000.00 in hundreds, twenty-two one ounce Suisse gold bars, and a cheap metal box that was locked. Jack took the whole box.

Jack missed the real valuables. Jack never fond the a safe behind the steel lockers in the indoor pool ares. That safe contained $500,000.00 in cash and over $1 million in jewelry and gold. The owner had planned an easy find to foil any burglars.

After scooping up the flowers and his black duffel bag, Jack went out the side door to the attached eight car garage. the car collection was to die for. There was a 1965 289 Ford

Cobra, a 1969 Ford Cobra Daytona fast back that obviously had been raced, a black four door Lincoln convertible with gorgeous red leather seats, a 350 Ford Cobra Mustang GT, an immaculate 1964 Ford Mustang convertible, and most incredibly, an original Ford GT40 which Henry Ford II used to beat Ferrari four consecutive times at LeMans from 1966 to 1969 including a 1-2-3 finish in 1966. The GT 40 alone was worth a million dollars.

There were three GULF oil signs and a functioning 1950s style Gulf gasoline pump.

Next to the first garage door was a duffel bag that was somewhat bigger than the one Jack carried. He liked the bag so he took the unopened bag with him even though it was heavy. He fled into the van and into the anonymity of traffic. Shortly after left the WINDY HILL driveway and merged onto the main road, he saw a new Ford Mustang GT. There was barely enough room in the Mustang's back seat for the couple's two Bull Mastiffs. The driver and passenger had just dropped off two duffel bags that were sold to a mid level dealer.

Two different duffel bags full of $100.00 bills were in the car's trunk. Jack waived to the passing Ford driver.

At home Jack bashed open the metal box with a hammer and flat bar, revealing an additional $10,000,00 and thirty-four packets of white powder. "This guy's an addict," he thought. Jack rubbed some of the powder on his upper lip confirming that it was cocaine. The owner of WINDY HILL actually never used drugs. He was a big time coke dealer.

Jack brought the duffel bag to a dumpster to unload the contents. Jack was really taken aback wen he opened the duffel. The bag was full of drugs. There were individually packaged bags containing one pound of cocaine each. The cocaine disturbed Jack. He knew that it was valuable but he didn't want to get caught with it and didn't know what to do with it. He also realized that the guy that he had robbed would be looking for him.

He visited his friend Pickins. Pickins quickly calculated that the duffel bag was worth $3,000,000,00. There were 100 one kilogram packsts that were worth $30,000.00 each. The duffel bag weighed about forty-five pounds. Pickins offered a 50/50 split with Jack.

"No, 25/75," said Jack.

One third/two thirds and you've got a deal," Pickins offered back.

"Deal. And you can keep the sample packets."

Jack kept the duffel bag and Pickins enjoyed the sample packets which he didn't share with anyone.

03/16/1979 KIETH AND ELAINE JOHNSON WOLD'S HOME

Dr. Kieth Wold's life was like one written for a movie script. He graduated from St. Paul's Academy and the University of North Dakota and UVM school of Medicine. He served the US Army in the South Pacific during World War Two in the medical corps. Dr. Wold and wife Elaine had a son and daughter.

Kieth Wold practiced ophthalmology in

Fort lauderdale where he preformed eye surgery. He was an avid yachtsman who participated in numerous ocean yacht races. He bred thoroughbred horses. Dr. Wold and his wife formed foundations and charitable trusts for the handicapped and disabled. His Wold Corporation managed business investments in agriculture, real estate and transportation.

In 1997 Elaine Johnson Wold was listed as the 342nd richest American, according to Forbes magazine, with a net worth of $560 million.

Elaine was one of six children of J. Steward Johnson I, who was the son of General Johnson (he was a WW II army tank commander), one of J&J's founders. Elaine's inherited wealth came from Band-Aids, Baby Oil, Baby Powder and many other medical and health products of the company that went public in 1944.

Elaine managed to avoid the fates of other J&J relatives: one died of cancer, one was paralyzed in a motorcycle accident, two died of a drug overdoses and one was fired from J&J.

Why Jack robbed the Wold residence is a mystery. Jack may have been suckered into believing, as Dick and Perry did in Truman Capote's book, In "Cold Blood", that the house had more valuables in it than it actuality had.

Jack didn't like the feel of the Wold's residence. The place was immense. Jack did like the long cobblestone driveway, and the perfect landscaping. There was a three car garage to the left of the drive and another three car garage next to the house. Jack liked the oiled teak garage doors. The rear view, from the pool area was beautiful open ocean. The pool itself had twelve Titanic style teak chaise lounges surrounding it. Jack liked the billiard room but disliked the house's furniture, the chandeliers, and the art work. He had never seen a kitchen as large as the Wold's. The kitchen was 80 feet long by 40 feet wide. It had a twelve burner gas stove at one end and a six burner stove at the other. Jack thought that the house was about as homey as a hospital.

The Wold's estate was secured with a state of the art security system that included weight, motion and heat sensors. Considering the security that the Wolds had, one would assume that the Wold's property would be immune to Jack and his ilk but it wasn't.

The 18,000 square foot house was so large that, at one point, Jack found himself lost. Two people lived in the house with eight bedrooms, and thirteen bathrooms. It had almost half an acre of floor space. Investigators never figured out how Jack avoided the security system. Jack and three associates absconding with around $1 million in jewelry cash and other valuables.

Jack always burglarized homes by himself but broke his own rules for the Wolds robbery by bringing three others with him. He expected the haul to be so big that he wouldn't be able to haul all the merchandize by himself. The take from the Wold mansion was around $1 million but it was almost all jewelry. Since Jack had to fence jewelry he got only 20% of the value. The $200,000.00 heist, split four ways was a meager haul for Jack and less for his assistants.

During the robbery one of the four intruders dropped a radio which had had its crystal replaced with one that would receive police broadcasts. A detective discovered the crystal and an investigation found that it had been purchased by Jack. Jack was caught, charged, prosecuted, and sentenced to Dade County Prison for fifteen years.

The terms jail and prison are sometimes used interchangeably since both are used to incarcerate people. Jail is generally run by local governments - towns, cities or counties. Jails usually house people for shorter periods of time whether they are convicted of a crime or awaiting trial and have not "made bail". Prisons are generally run by states or federal authorities. Inmates in prison almost exclusively have been convicted of a crime(s). Prison populations generally have been sentenced to one or more years. People in federal prisons have committed a federal crime.

In 1979 Jack was found guilty of burglary and sentenced to fifteen years in prison by a Broward County Florida judge. Florida prison, for Jack, was better than for some other convicts.

Burglary is a crime that is respected by

other inmates and tolerable for prison guards. Jack was able to gain other inmates protection and favors by luring them with promises of partnership in future burglaries. The convicts would enjoy the hours of planning future capers with him. Jack conned the convicts. Spending seven and a half years in the sweaty Florida prison was, however, not a walk in the park. Burglary was what Jack knew and what he did, so he returned to his profession, as do many inmates, upon release.

FIRST INCARCERATION

Being arrested is an awful experience whether its standing next to one's car after failing a Driving While Intoxicated test or when a SWAT team comes to your house, with automatic weapons, helmets, and bullet proof vests. It will not be a good day for anyone who is arrested. A SWAT team came for Jack. The visit did not end well.

Jack was at his Florida house when, from his security camera, he first saw a SWAT team member jumping off his porch. He looked outside and there seemed to be swarms of them, all dressed in black. His street and adjoining blocks were cordoned off. Then he got a telephone call from the police captain. Jack had met the captain and recognized his name.

"Jack we have a warrant for your arrest. Will you let us in so that we don't have to arrest you in front of your neighbors?"

"I'll come out."

The captain wanted to enter the house so that he could look around. He had an arrest warrant but didn't, as yet, have a search warrant.

Jack walked out the front door with his hands up assuming that his greeting would be polite.

"DOWNONYOURKNEESWITHYOUR HANDSBEHINDYOURHEAD, ONYOURKNEES, DOWNNOW" There was no longer any friendly conversation.

He was quickly handcuffed and his legs were shackled. Then he was thrown face down in his driveway, frisked and put in the back seat of a police cruiser. Jack knew his jovial charm was not going to serve him well his situation, so he sat in the police cruiser silently.

At the local police station Jack was asked some questions that made him shudder. He knew that the predicament was dire.

"We found your radio at the Wold residence, do you want to admit to the burglary? Do you have any of the jewelry at your house?"

Jack's "I want my lawyer," response stopped the questions.

Jack was never read his Miranda Rights.

All Jack's assets were rapidly taken under Civil Judicial Forfeiture. Jack's houses in Maine and Florida were confiscated. His two boats, his two airplanes, the $200,000.00 that was buried in his back yard, five cars, and his beloved Hughes 300C helicopter were suddenly not his anymore. A total of just under $6 million was taken as forfeiture. As always in such cases, law enforcement wondered what had happened to the rest of the money.

Jack was soon penniless, his friends fled like rats on a sinking ship, and his girlfriend went on to another carnival.

Jack's fingerprints were taken as were photographs of his face for mug shots. The mug shots appeared in the local papers. Mug shots never look good. The bail bondsman took two hours to get to the station. Jack was shocked by the bail - one million dollars - cash. Only immediate payment would allow his freedom. Since he didn't have that much cash laying around he was taken to the county jail.

Jack's figured that someday he might need bail money. He had previously buried $200,000.00 in his back yard, just incase. He should have buried a lot more money or, in retrospect, not robbed the Wold home. The buried money was easily found by a black lab.

Jack sat in a group of chairs that were locked together. Sixteen seats with all but two occupied. Processing would take three hours. Each time someone left for lock up, more would come in to be processed.

His wallet, "his" new Breitling watch, keys and pocket change were put in an manila envelope after which he was again fingerprinted and photographed. The holding cell had no furniture and only a drain on the floor to collect anything that came out of an inmate's body (yes, Jack became an inmate); piss, shit, puke or blood all went into the drain in the floor's center. The cell's floor tapered gently so that anything fluid would flow into the drain. Nothing was allowed in the holding cell - no food, water, nor books were allowed. Piece of mind would never find its way into the hell of a cell.

"What are you in for," was the topic of conversation in the holding cell.

Before too long Jack was given a single cell to the left of the intake desk. The cell had a toilet and a sink, a thin pad to cover the steel bed slab, and a blanket. Everything Jack did was observed. He might as well take a shit in Times Square for the lack of privacy. His narrow view from the cell enabled him to watch a pretty young woman in the women's intake area, squat over the drain to pee. It was not erotic. Even Jack felt sorry for her. He figured that she must be in for DWI or prostitution. The next morning the pee girl was let out of the holding cell. She rummaged through her purse until she found deodorant which she applied from under her blouse. Somebody apparently made bail for the dear girl but most assuredly, the young woman's bail was far less than Jack's $1 million.

Sleeping was difficult because of the noise and the overhead light that was constantly on. Meals were slipped through a slot in the cell bars. Each time a cell door clanked shut was a reminder that he was in jail and he had no idea for how long it would be.

There was nothing to read, no TV or radio, no one to talk with so Jack peeled paint. He peeled paint off the walls, off the floor and off the steel bunk. Peeling the paint gave him some semblance of purpose. A guard yelled at him for peeling the paint.

"What are you a moron?"

"What are you going to do throw me in jail?" Jack shot back. He didn't like being called a moron.

"Why are you doing that?" the guard continued.

"I have nothing else to do."

"You are entitled to a bible."

The guard delivered a brand new bible.

Jack looked at the ceiling and asked out loud, "Is that a sign?"

No one answered.

Jack was starting to loose IT.

On the second day he was taken for a video arraignment. He was charged with second degree burglary, possession of stolen merchandise and possession of burglarious tools. Other charges were pending. Things didn't look good. The arraignment judge kept his bail at one million dollars.

THE INFIRMARY - CELL MATE #1

Jack didn't know the jail system so he told the intake nurse that he was depressed hoping to get some sympathy and special treatment. Jack didn't even know what might be available but he hoped for something more accommodating. Because he said that he was depressed, the nurse assigned him to the infirmary and he was put on suicide watch. The infirmary was better than his first cell because there was one other person to talk with.

Tim was an average looking guy of medium height and build. He skin color was darker than a paper bag but not "purple Black". Tim was well spoken as might be expected of someone educated in a New England prep school.

Tim would sometimes talk about things that Jack was clueless about. Once Tim mentioned sugar subsidies that Florida growers received but stopped because he felt that Jack had no idea what he was talking about. Although both men had graduated from high school, Tim was far better educated.

Tim wore tan prison clothes because he had been convicted. Jack wore grey because he had not been tried. The men were born one week apart.

Tim, like Jack, was adopted. His family, an older white couple owned a large farm that grew produce. The family had also adopted Tim's sister. Tim said that the couple really only wanted his sister but his sister wouldn't go without him. The farm was a "dirt farm" not a cattle farm. The family had a farm stand and sold produce to restaurants. Tim's adopted parents died and left the farm to Tim and his sister.

The family's farming business was hard and the whole family worked long hours. Tim's portion of the family's estate sale was put into a trust so that he couldn't blow the inheritance on cocaine.

Tim got busted for cocaine trafficking and was waiting to be transported to a federal penitentiary. Jack figured that Tim must have crossed state lines for the feds to have intervened.

Sociologists who dispute the nature/nurture issue would have had great interest in the cellmates.

SIMILARITIES:

. Both men were adopted by white families.

. Both men had younger sisters who were adopted and became successful.

. Both men graduated from high school.

. Both men's fathers had their own business.

. Neither man found substantial employment after high school.
. Both owned two homes.

. Both men did well in their "professions".

. Both men would return to their former professions after release.
. Both men were smart but not smart enough not to get caught.

. Both men lost everything to criminal forfeiture.

DIFFERENCES:
. Jack is white. Tim is Black.
. Tim's sister is a biological sister. Jack's sister

came from a different family.

. Tim's sister became an pediatrician. Jack's sister married a minister.

. Jack barely graduated from public school. Tim graduated from a prestigious preparatory
    school.

. Tim worked on the farm. Jack never did "hard work".

. Tim was a drug dealer. Jack was a burglar.

. Tim read magazines while Jack only looked at the pictures.

. Jack got sentenced to 15 years. Tim got 10 to 12 years.

. Tim was busted in a sting operation. Jack's partner left the radio that led to his arrest.

. Tim referred to his parents as his step parents. Jack simply called his step parents his parents.

Jack liked Tim and they talked a great deal. Two days later Tim was taken at 2:00 AM to be flown to a federal penitentiary in Arizona where he would spend the next five years if he got time off for good behavior.

Tim had showed Jack some of the prison's

ropes: After pissing one had to wipe the toilet clean (the toilet "seat" was part of the stainless steel toilet). When one of them has to shit the other must look out the bars. There is no door or even walls around prison toilets. Hand washing after toilet use is mandatory because infections are rampant in prisons. Prison sex will most likely kill you.

Tim told Jack the canteen schedule and how much a telephone call cost - $2.75 for a local call and $5.25 for long distance for one minute. Telephone charges are deducted from the inmate's canteen account. Having cash in prison is a serious violation that will result in good time being lost. The only telephones, for sixty men, were in the cell block. One phone could be listened into by the guards and the other secure line that was solely to be used for contacting one's attorney.

THE BANK ROBBER - CELL MATE #2

Manipulative personalities don't do well in areas like the infirmary or solitary confinement since they have no one to manipulate. Jack did not like to be alone.

No new cell mate came for four days. Jack's only human contact was when breakfast came at 7:00 AM, lunch at 12:30 PM and dinner at 5:00 PM. There were fourteen hours between dinner and breakfast. Beds, that sat on the floor in the infirmary, were made of molded plastic with no padding. The beds were designed so that they could not be used as a weapon, bed comfort was secondary. The only daylight came from two small barred windows which were six feet from the floor. The overhead lights were on 24 hours a day. There was no recreation, no television, no religious services, no AA, and there was no hope.

Jack's new cell mate, Wayne, was four years younger than Jack. Wayne was not good looking and looked greasy, as though he had not showered in a long, long time. Wayne's long hair was was brown but probably would have looked lighter after a shampoo. Wayne was overweight and his muscles had no tone.

Wayne robbed a bank which impressed the hell out of Jack. Jack knew that he didn't have the balls to rob a bank. After learning the penalty for bank robbery and the meager amount of an average bank robbery, Jack knew that being a burglar was a better profession. Besides, all bank robberies are a federal offense and Jack didn't want the feds on is tail.

The new roommate mostly slept. He was not a talker and showed no interest in Jack's line of work. When he was awake Wayne stared at the ceiling silently.

"I'm Jack," he initiated the conversation extending his hand. Jack had not forgotten his polite upbringing and the society that he left behind.

"Wayne," he was surprised by the offering of a handshake - handshakes were not a custom in prison. Wayne's handshake was a wet noodle.

"What are you in for?"

"I robbed a bank."

"No shit. Jack spun around facing the

ceiling in disbelief. You robbed - a - bank!"

Jack had to have the details.

"Where?"

"A branch on route one."

"Did you use a gun?"

Jack figured that they might have a nice conversation about guns.

"No, no. Even a toy gun will add another fifteen."

"What did you say? Give me all your money."

"No. I just showed the teller a note. Customers always give tellers pieces of paper and if you don't say anything the teller can't recognize your voice. You're not supposed to give them the note because the feds can trace the finger prints, ink, and paper and it can be used as evidence."

"What did you use for a getaway car?" Jack hoped that the getaway vehicle might be some souped up machine and that there might have been a high speed getaway and they might be able to talk about cars.

"No car."

No car? What did you use, a bicycle?"

"Walked."

"Walked?"

"Walked to the hotel across the street."

"How did they catch you?"

"Somebody saw me enter the hotel."

"So you didn't even get to spend the money?"

"In the three hours before I got caught, I smoked $2,000.00 of crack."

That was too much for Jack because he was so against drug use. But worse, throwing away $2,000.00 in three hours with nothing to show for it was inexcusable.

Some conversations went more smoothly.

"So what prompted you to rob the bank?"

"I figured that they had money. I figured right."

"Most people put money in before they take it out you realize?" Jack joked.

"I do realize that but since I never had any money to put in they simply might front some to me."

"It just wouldn't occur to me to walk into a bank and "suggest" that the teller should hand over her cash."

"That's probably because your father never robbed a bank."

"Your father robbed a bank?"

"My father and my brother. In fact my father robbed two banks - both successfully."

"He didn't get caught?"

"My father didn't get caught but my brother did."

"How? How did your father get away with it?"

"Like you, my father planned his heists. His planning was meticulous. He robbed two banks in downtown Boston in 1970 on back to back Friday afternoons. In bank robbery, the getaway is everything and the execution is secondary but still very important. If the robber gets out of the bank his chances of being caught are halved. Before he started the robbery, my father had three stacks of money. He had twenty-five fives, fifty ones, and thirty-five ones. He entered both banks at precisely 4:45 pm. He parked his Honda 50 . . ."

"I had a Honda 50. Sorry to interrupt."

"He parked his Honda 50 on the sidewalk outside the bank's side door and left the Honda running. He always chose a bank with a side door because some front doors can be remotely locked. Once inside he showed two tellers his note, remember I told you to never give the teller the note. Then he unfolded two nylon duffel bags, giving one to each teller. Then he told the tellers to 'fill it - the faster you fill it the faster I'll be gone. If you put a die packet in, one of us may never leave'."

"Once the duffel bags were full, my father would take the stack of fives and throw them in the air. Customers flocked to pick up the fivers and chaos ensued. He left the banks by the side door and got onto the Honda, heading the wrong way down a one way street. At the first intersection he would toss the fifty one dollar bills in the air. Chaos again with a huge traffic jam. People didn't look at anything except the money. Dad's getaway took him through Boston traffic during a Friday rush hour. He sped between the backed up cars with ease. Even if cops were chasing him they couldn't get through the traffic jams. Dad never had to use the third stack of money. He didn't need to."

"I love a well planned crime. why didn't your father rob more banks/"

"Dad had the numbers all worked out. He figured that the Feds would treat one robbery as a single desperate act. A second robbery with the same MO would get serious FBI attention. After two robberies the feds would assign a task force, so getting caught would substantially escalate. Remember, every bank robbery is a Federal offense and all bank robberies are considered dangerous to the public and to bank employees. Dad quit while he was ahead."

"What happened to your brother?"

"I should have learned from him," Wayne confessed as he shook his head.

"Another dumb move?"

"Dumb? Simply moronic. First he had a gun. He thought that because it wasn't loaded it wouldn't count as an armed robbery. He pointed it at the teller's head and the teller promptly fainted. Then he tried to climb over the teller's window but he was so out of shape that he fell and broke his arm. The bank guard calmly walked over and put his gun to my brother's head. Game over. My brother was never destined for greatness. He's in USP Leavenworth. The good thing is that I probably won't have to go to Leavenworth. The Feds don't like to have family members in the same hole."

After that interesting discussion Wayne slipped back into a semi coma. No matter how he tried Jack couldn't get Wayne to converse. Wayne, like Tim, was whisked away in the middle of the night. He was taken to USP Allenwood.

Wayne stayed for only two days. Jack didn't miss him but the boredom of the cell's tile walls and total lack of stimulation was getting to him. Intake had promised that he would be assigned to a cell block in two days but ten had passed.

Jack finally told a guard that he didn't want his lunch and that he was going on a hunger strike until he was released from the infirmary. Ten minutes later a social worker came, apologized for the oversight, and told him he would be placed in a cell block the next day.

CELL BLOC "A"

Jack was finally given a bunk in cell block A. The heat in Block A was stifling. The previous cells that he was in had some air-conditioning because administrative offices were a part of the open section of the infirmary. The cell blocks had no air-conditioning and the air inside did not move. Block A was for nonviolent offenders who had yet to be tried.

Lawyers for offenders like Jack frequently start out with great effort then fizzle. Plea bargaining is all such lawyers can offer. Public defenders (PDs) don't even consider trying a case unless the charges are a total fabrication. PDs simply negotiate a plea bargain. Trials for accused offenders who have PDs are rare.

Jack took a fifteen year plea bargain with the understanding that he could be released in seven and a half years if he qualified for good behavior. One had to be fairly offensive to not get good behavior credit. Jack would soon be transferred from his jail cell to prison.

On February 13, 1987 John Arthur MacLean entered six "counter pleas". The court reported six convictions by plea - adjudicated. The court ordered his incarceration effective 3/27/80 effective 12:00 Am. He was sentenced to a maximum of 15 years - 0 months - 0 days.

Jack's criminal records from Florida and Arizona are in the appendix at the end of this book.

Cell blocks are similar to those depicted in movies and on TV since most are actually filmed in real prisons. Jack would spend the next seven and a half years in the two story thirty cell hell. The cells surrounded the day area where he would eat, play cards, watch TV, and do his time.

Time is not on your side in jail. Every day just brings another day without sunshine or joy.

Everything in jail and prison is designed so that it cannot be used as a weapon. Cheap razors have to be returned within ten minutes. Any razors that are not returned would searched for and found by the guards. An inmate who failed to return a razor would be sent to the hole. Shaving is allowed every other day unless a court appearance is scheduled. Toothbrushes fit on the tip of one's finger and the bristles fall off almost automatically. The two bunkbeds are a thick steel tray that is bolted to the concrete wall. There was no cute little desk and chair for inmates to write to their mother or girlfriend. There was a steel tray which also was bolted to the wall.

Jail food is eaten with a spork. There are no knives, not even plastic knives. Meals must be eaten in ten minutes. No food is allowed in cells. Fourteen hours pass between supper and breakfast.

Prices for canteen products are three or four times grocery store prices. Telephone calls are extremely expensive and phones can only be used at specific times. Sixty or more inmates share only one or two pay phones.

If there is a disturbance or miscalculation in inmate count, a lockdown ensues and lasts until the problem is solved. Showers are short and only somewhat private. Toilet use is timed so that one's cellmate is not in the cell so that it can be private.

No inmate is allowed in any cell other than his own. Beds must always be made if prisoners are not laying in them. Blankets can only cover inmates at night.

All inmate mail is read and censored by

guards. The stamps are removed in case LSD is under the stamp. It has been known to happen.

Visitors have to be preauthorized. Visits are through a thick glass partition with each person using a phone. Jack, as with many of the cellmates, had very few visitors. Most inmates didn't want anyone they knew to see them in jail. Everything in jail was degrading.

There is no sanctuary and no peace. Time is killed and never enjoyed.

CELL BLOCK "A" RESIDENTS

A guy dressed in an orange sat on the stairs that led to the upper cells. The color of inmate's prison garb caught Jack's eye. The man in orange was about forty, slim, with athletic build. He exuded an air of confidence. He also smiled, which is a rare prison behavior.

In a different setting, with different clothing the orange man could have passed as a car salesman or even a mid level professional.

Jack was curious about the orange garb but it was the guy's smile made him approachable.

"Why are you dressed in orange?" questioned Jack.

"I'm going to Dade County and we wear orange there."

"Why are you here?"

"I got caught here so they dressed me in Dade colors to identify me. I'll be transferred in two days."

"What did you do to get caught?"

"Identity theft. You?"

"Burglary. Second degree."

"Whose identity did you steal?"

"Hundreds of people's. Maybe a thousand."

"Really?"

"We'd drive around and grab mail from mail boxes. We'd take any credit card applications and send them in all filled out. Then we would keep checking the mailboxes until the cards came in. If you ever see a permanent magic marker mark on your mail box you're in trouble since we mark the mailboxes for identification. One card alone had twenty-five grand in credit."

"Where did you get the information to fill out the applications?"

"We made it up mostly. I have a source for social security numbers."

"Was it a good scam?"

"Three of us, two guys and a girl, did a half million a year each. We did it for three years. It was a pretty good scam. We worked hard. I'll also be facing counterfeiting charges."

Jack was enthralled. He had never even thought about counterfeiting (he had't thought about robbing banks or identity theft either). Jail can certainly be a place for criminals to get an education in crime. Inmates don't learn how to be better people, they learn how to be better criminals.

"How did you print the money?"

"First you have to get a superior quality copier. Then you get top grade 100% rag paper, rag contains no wood pulp. One hundred gsm, gramage it's called in the business, paper is necessary. After printing you spray the money with hair spray to fool those detector pens that every check out clerk uses. It's dangerous because it's a federal offense. The feds can make you do twenty-five. We made $100s and $20s. I mostly pushed them on drug dealers. We, of course paid for the copiers with the credit cards that were stolen. There is an encryption on every copy produced so we didn't want the encryption traced to us."

The guy's wife and daughter were also in jail for breaking and entering and attempted burglary.

Jack confessed, "I'll have to meet them some time."

Other guys were just stupid. One guy stole railroad tracks and sold them as scrap metal. Not only did he get caught but it was a lot of work.

Most of the inmates were in for theft, drug dealing, and assaults. Actually, all the inmates were in jail for being stupid.

Gregg, in particular was a stupid little shit whose crimes were distasteful to the other inmates. Barely eighteen Gregg was facing a menu of charges including arson, car theft, and assault. His parents had given him a Corvette his senior year in high school in anticipation of graduating. Gregg promptly quit school. His parents made the mistake of buying and registering the car in Gregg's name.

Gregg became a professional car thief who would strip parts off the stolen vehicles and sell the parts. Then he would burn the cars.

After his arraignment Gregg shuffled beck to Block A.

"Judge said I was a menace to society. What an asshole."

Manny shot back, "You ARE a menace to society."

"You judging me coke head?"

"I am judging you. You didn't have to burn the cars."

"I didn't want my prints on them."

"They found your prints anyway. Didn't they?"

Gregg sulked to his cell.

One day the carts came for lunch. Jack got to the cart and looked around it.

"What do you want MacLean?" demanded one corrections officer.

"I'm looking for my lunch. I ordered a porterhouse steak."

A CO walked Jack to his cell, "No lunch asshole. You think you're funny?"

Jack didn't even get his slightly colored, slightly sweetened "Kool Aid".

Once a week the inmates would get an orange. The orange peels were valuable because the orange rinds could be used to make Constant Comment-like tea.

The day area of Cell Block A held some relief from the torture of the infirmary. There was a TV, which the young guys controlled. There were board games and cards but it was mostly too hot to do anything. There were books but Jack didn't read.

Fortunately, there was always someone to talk with in the cell block. Jack learned everyone's trade. Since Jack was the top earner, many of the inmates sought his counsel. Trade talk was always intimate and discussed in hushed voices. Jack never divulged the real key to his success - his ability to open locked doors, disable security systems, and open safes.

Some men walked continuously in a figure eight over a predetermined course, never stopping or talking to anyone. Others never left their cells.

If there were clocks, they would have ticked slowly.

MR. INSANE - JAIL MATE #3

Jack's first cell mate was a younger white guy who had a good physique. Only one quarter of the jail's population was white but the guards paired cellmates by race whenever possible to avoid racial conflict. Although they shared a 7 X 10 foot cell for almost a year Jack never knew his cellmates name and never addressed him by name.

The cellmate asked, "What are you in for?"

"Burglary," answered Jack. He was not ready to expound on his exploits.

"You?"

"Attempted murder."

The cellmate's response got Jack's attention. Cellblock A was, he thought, for nonviolent offenders.

"Why are you in A?"

"I'm still awaiting trial. I haven't been convicted of anything."

"Who did you try to off?"

"My stepfather. He came home drunk and started to beat up my mother. I threw him down the stairs and slit his throat. He lived."

Jack immediately considered getting a change of address but had no idea of how he could accomplish getting his bunk changed. What if he got someone even crazier? Cell mate #3 had a very muscular build. He also had "bitch tits" which Jack knew was frequently a result of steroid use. Jack also knew that steroid use can result in 'roid rage.

Jack came to the stark realization that each and every person, that he was now living with, had some degree of instability. All the guys that he lived with were in jail for a reason. With a new cell mate he could go from the frying pan into the fire.

"How long have you been here?" wondered Jack.

"Almost three years."

"What? Three years and you haven't had a trial?"

"I've refused a PD since they're a joke. I've been handling my own case."

Jack realized that the cellmate only had one oar in the water. The guy didn't have the ability to defend himself for a speeding ticket let alone an attempted murder charge. Three years and hadn't had a trial. Jack realized that the years awaiting trial really didn't matter as the "time served" would be taken off his sentence. Maybe the guy did know what he was doing and was merely avoiding being placed in one of the cellblocks for violent offenders and being sent to state prison.

To make matter worse, Yugo Danny, told Jack that his cellmate didn't try to kill his stepfather for beating up his mother but rather the cellmate had "mother issues".

The cellmate displayed a number of other behaviors that were completely crazy.

During lockdown the guy would pace around the cell declaring the ability to speak in a foreign language (unspecified which country or language).

"Yasippintytubotmamzierobbotwinniemab b . . ." he would spout sometimes for an hour.

Jack never knew wether the guy really thought such gibberish was actually a foreign language or if he was just trying to be entertaining. Jack was not entertained.

Cellmate #3 also claimed to have been hired by Yamaha to race "Quads" - four wheel motorcycles. He wasn't able to tell Jack how long his contract was for however. The guy was a mental mess who lived in a reality free zone. He eventually took a plea and was sent to another cell block and eventually to prison.

FROM JAIL TO PRISON

Jack was escorted to the hallway just outside the administrative desk. The guard desk was inside the cellblock area in jail. Five other inmates and Jack were lined up against the wall, handcuffed and leg shackled. All six were patted down from head to toe including body cavities. They were then handcuffed in pairs.

The ride to court was terribly hot. Once the duck walking group with leg chains walked up the stairs the air conditioned court provided some relief. It would be the last relief from heat that Jack would get for seven and a half years.

Witnesses and other court attendees stared and gasped at the six inmates. The six inmates appearance with obvious prison uniforms, handcuffs, and leg chains were anxiety provoking for the court's attendees. The guards unlocked the prisoner's leg chains but left each man individually handcuffed.

Judge Mathews asked Jack if he understood the charges and if he understood that he would face imprisonment Florida State Prison. Jack affirmed that he understood. Jack and his lawyer stood before Judge Mathews to receive the fifteen year sentence which came as no shock since the sentence was the basis of the plea bargain.

After all six men were sentenced, they

were taken back to the paddy wagon for the two hour trip to the Big House. The men sat on steel benches that faced the wagon's center isle. Lap belts were buckled by the guards with a warning to the prisoners to not unbuckle. They were again handcuffed in pairs and leg chains were refastened.

There was a limited view of the outside from the small rear window and through the driver's window. There was some satisfaction in being able to view the real world. Jack would not see the outside world again for seven and a half years.

Upon arrival at the state prison, the driver remotely opened a large garage door, drove inside, and remotely closed the door. All six of the paddy wagon's occupants sat until four guards arrived carrying automatic rifles. One unarmed guard unlocked the paddy wagon's rear door allowing all six prisoners to exit. No one rushed because time was only something to kill.

Since prisoners had been known to acquire contraband in courtrooms all six men were thoroughly searched and had all their body cavities examined once again. An anal search is as dehumanizing as one can imagine. Prison guards did the examination more thoroughly than the jail guards. The men's grey prison clothes were exchanged for tan. The men were photographed, fingerprinted, and once again, they waited.

Jack was the second to be assigned a cell. Seven and a half years, with good behavior, was going to be an eternity. It was 1979 and he would not be freed until 1986 at the very earliest.

The guard's desk in prison was outside the cellblock unlike jail's desk which was inside the cellblock. Jack realized that the prison population would be a much tougher and more desperate group. The guards' desk area was elevated five feet above ground floor it offered a commanding view of the cellblock and the height offered protection from inmates. Unlike jail, all inmates in prison had been convicted and sentenced. There are no choirboys in prison. Everyone in the prison had been found guilty of a crime and had been sentenced to at least one year.

The prison did offer some relief from the daily cell lockup. There was an outside recreation area that consisted of dirt, just dirt - no grass, no trees but it was at least outside. Weight lifting was monopolized by Black prisoners with a few white ones who had earned entry by beating up tough Black ones.

Whites, Blacks, and Hispanic prisoners grouped in separate areas. The majority of the inmates were Black with White and Hispanic about equal in number. White inmates did not make eye contact with other races unless they wanted to get beaten.

There was some status according to one's crime. Lifers convicted of multiple murderers were most feared and therefore most respected. Lifers didn't have anything to loose. Burglars and drug dealers were about equal. Jack's status was elevated by the shear number of burglaries and the huge amounts that he had stolen. Life in prison for rapists and pedophiles was pure hell.

Jack got a job in the prison laundry. Six days a week he took clothes out of the dryers, folded the clothes and sorted them according to size. The job was for new prisoners since no one wanted the additional heat from the dryers to further the torture from the hot Florida days. Jack did the work and took some pride in the job. The work paid fifteen and a half cents per hour.

Jack discovered other activities to help with the long days of incarceration. Jack attended AA meetings although he never drank or took drugs. He went to church. Although he graduated from high school he took GED classes.

In order to be enrolled in GED classes an inmate had to pass an interview. The teacher wanted only motivated students. Ms Jackson, the frumpy forty year old teacher, initially rejected Jack.

"You're a high school graduate. You don't need a GED."

"I can read words but I can't really read," pleaded Jack.

Ms Jackson had experience with men like Jack and was sympathetic with their plight. Jack was allowed to enter the GED program.

Jack was given a mimeographed short story and asked to read it.

"What did the main character do for work?" asked Ms Jackson.

"I don't know."

"What was the main character's name?"

"Bobby."

Ms Jackson realized what Jack's problem was and knew some techniques on how to work around it. She knew that the learning disability could not be solved but it could be overcome with some effort.

"What I want you to do is read the last paragraph of the story first. Then read the next to last paragraph and so on, until you get to the first paragraph. Then read it again from first to last."

Ms Jackson was anxious because some students got really confused by her instructions. Jack understood her instructions.

Jack bounded into the classroom the next day. "Bobby was a migrant worker from Jamaica who picked apples in New Hampshire." For the first time in his life Jack was really able to read text and not relegated to reading mere words.

Ms Jackson was amazed at the results of her efforts. She was proud of herself and the happiest she had ever been in her somewhat thankless job.

With Ms Jackson's help Jack quickly progressed from grammar school level to junior high level and finally to high school level. Jack began to read books and magazines on his own. Jack's new found ability to read made jail much more tolerable. A new world opened up to him. Magazines became more than just pictures. Jack enjoyed picking out the flaws in the books he enjoyed the most - detective novels.

Ms Jackson started dressing more stylishly. She let her hair grow longer and shed her glasses for contact lenses. She became almost attractive. Jack even noticed a hint of makeup and lipstick. Perfume?

Ms Jackson worked diligently with Jack and he flourished. She worried about Jack's future upon his release. She learned that Jack had no marketable skills and that his family had cut off contact with him. She frequently witnessed inmates who after release had no alternative but to return to their previous life of crime.

Jack was an expert in one thing - burglary. Burglary, however, is not a marketable trade. Unless . . .

"Jack, what about writing a book about your escapades?"

"I have no idea how to write a book, Ms Jackson."

"I can help you. I'll walk you through it and help you get it published."

"Well the statute of limitations has expired for my burglaries so that is no longer an issue. But won't the proceeds of the book be used for restitution?"

"Your victims might try to attach your earnings but according to a lawyer I talked with, any profits from your book would not be a direct result of your crimes. The lawyer also advised that your book be written as a "how not to be a victim".

"My book." Jack never in his life thought that he would hear those words spoken.

Jack and Ms Jackson worked long and hard on the 177 page book, "Secrets of a Super-thief". Jack wrote every day for fifteen months.

Ms Jackson and Jack became very close. As Jack got more and more studious and Ms Jackson got more and more attractive.

Jack was only able to stretch the book to thirty-five thousand words (most books have seventy thousand word minimums). He added sixteen pages of sketches and sample signs to stretch the book. With three quarter inch side margins and one inch top and bottom margins he had barely enough content for a publisher.

Ms Jackson brought in chocolate chip cookies and root beer barrels. Jack brought his smile.

MANNY - CELL MATE #4

Manny was a young, handsome Puerto Rican kid who was born and raised in Lewiston Maine. He had a kind of pretty baby face with well proportioned features. His looks made him a chick magnet. Jack and Manny talked a lot about their childhoods.

"We ate a lot of government surplus food: blocks of processed cheese, cans of vegetables with plain white labels, and powdered milk. I didn't know that milk came in cartons until I was six. Some nights all we had was corn flakes that came in big white boxes. Some nights we didn't have even powdered milk for the cereal and had to eat it with water. I used to not eat breakfast some mornings so that my sisters had enough food. We knew where every soup kitchen in Lewiston was and which churches had food pantries. All five kids would lug food home. School breakfasts and lunches saved me."

"We wore second hand donated clothes. The only time we saw a doctor was at the emergency room. Dentistry consisted of getting our teeth pulled."

"We had a two bedroom, third floor walkup in Lewiston. My mother, Maryann, had her own room, my four sisters shared a room, and I slept in the living room. We were always on the verge of eviction. Sometimes the landlord would come into the apartment demanding rent and Maryann and he would go into the kitchen and close the door for a half hour."

"I'm the oldest. Maryann had me when she was fourteen. My four sisters were born six years apart. I had a lot of "uncles" who slept over. They came and went."

"Maryann was always lugging us around to welfare, WIC, churches, and city hall to beg for assistance."

"Children's Services was always threatening to take us away but never did. Maryann is an alcoholic but she would do any chemicals that were offered. She loved coke. When she told social services that she was considering having another child, the city agreed to pay for her sterilization. It was hush hush."

"Why do you call her Maryann?" asked Jack.

"She didn't want anyone to know that I was her son. Our age difference was not great. She told people that I was her brother. She was pretty when she was young but the drugs and booze have done a job on her."

"She was never ashamed of our poverty

but I was. Poverty hung on me like an old man's coat. I hated it."

"How did you start dealing coke?"

"My mother's boyfriend stashed bricks of coke in the bedroom closet. He would paddle lock the door but I just removed the hinge pins. The guy was a total scum bag. Never as much as bought me a baseball. I stole his coke and replace the powder by cutting it with a combination of aspirin and saccharin. Sometimes I added No Doze. Pretty soon I was buying the cut in volume. I bought my own damn baseball. And glove."

"The guy finally figured out what I was doing. His customers were complaining about the quality of his shit. Instead of beating me up, he started beating up Maryann. He stopped when I knifed him in his side. I surprised the shit out of both of us. I left the knife in his side which probably kept him from bleeding to death. He grabbed his coke and stumbled out of the apartment never to be seen again. There was a lot of blood. I had saved enough money to be able to buy at mid level. The profits weren't as good but the scum bag was gone."

Jack told Manny about his go-cart, Honda, MG, and Corvette. Manny had no idea of what an MG was nor could he imagine why anyone would want one. Manny liked to hear about the number of bedrooms and bathrooms in the house on Hanscom Ave. A private pool, a garage, and a lawn that had to be mowed sounded like heaven to Manny.

Neither Jack's nor Manny's mothers ever worked at a traditional job. To Manny, Jack's life in Reading sounded much more appealing than Jack's life in Florida.

"Are you going to be deported back to Puerto Rico?" Jack asked.

"What do you mean?"

"Since you were convicted of a felony they can deport you right?

"Jack, you're the one who graduated from high school but you really have some gaps in your education. Puerto Rico is a US Territory. It is part of the United States. Puerto Ricans can come to the continental United States at will. We got citizenship in 1917. Puerto Ricans can't vote for president though."

"Well I'm embarrassed," admitted Jack.

Both men discussed their arrests. Jack explained that he was traced by the chip in his hand held radio that was left at the Johnson & Johnson heiress's residence.

"To make matters worse, we got mostly jewelry. Jewelry has to be fenced so our take wasn't great anyway."

Manny had driven from Maine to Florida in order to pick up a cocaine shipment. Manny's Miami coke buy was successful, so he headed back to Maine. Manny, however, was shy on cash so he tried to not get a motel. He stopped at a Walmart parking lot for a nap. He was awakened after an hour by four Georgia State Police cruisers and eight state cops who had guns pointed at him. The 6:00 news reported that Manny had fourteen pounds of cocaine in his car. At $35.00 per gram, 28 grams per ounce, and 16 ounces per pound, the street value of Manny's coke was $220,000.00. Since the coke cost Manny $55,000.00, he looked foreword to a hefty profit even if he had to wholesale part of it.

Manny didn't get to see any profits.

Jack finally allowed himself to brag about his book to his cell mate Manny.

"We're going to print this week. Too bad I can't do a book tour. Too bad I won't be able to tour with Ms Jackson."

"Jack, sit on the bed," instructed Manny.

"What?"

"You know what she is right?"

"What do you mean, 'what she is'?"

Jack was ready to hit Manny if he said something disingenuous about Ms Jackson. Manny saw Jack's fist clench. Manny walked over and put his hand gently on Jack's shoulder.

"Jack. She's a nun."

Jack stared at Manny in disbelief. In the year and a half that he and Ms Jackson had worked together on his book, she had given him no indication that she was a nun. Jack was crushed and angry. But it made sense.

"I figured that she must have been recently divorced since she had an indentation on her ring finger."

"Nuns wear a wedding ring because

they're married to God."

"No shit."

"She must have removed the ring before coming in every day. What you don't know about Catholics could fill your next book."

"How could I not know?"

The book got published. Ms Jackson left the convent and became Melissa. She quit working at the prison and took a job in a private school. She never married but she adopted a five year old girl. She lived (fairly) happily ever after. Jack and Ms Jackson never saw each other again. Jack missed her.

Manny was the best cellmate Jack had in his seven and a half years in prison. Manny was a genuinely nice guy who happened to make his living by selling drugs.

Despite a plea bargain that was supposed to be 364 days in jail, the judge sentenced Manny to 366 days in prison. That's how Manny got to be Jack's cell mate for a year and a day.

Manny had a son with his girlfriend. He actually had three children with three different girlfriends. In order to support his offspring he dealt cocaine, which he did somewhat successfully. Manny had, however, already spent half of his adult life in prison. He was only twenty-six years old yet was a typical revolving door criminal. Manny did not know why he had not been sentenced to life for his third strike offense. Before his recent incarceration he had already been in prison four times.

The one thing Jack didn't like about Manny was his hair, which was abundant and curly. Jack occasionally found Manny's hair on his bunk and would exclaim, "Pubic hair!" - which it actually did look like.

Manny disliked Jack's snoring. They got along.

Manny didn't want to become a burglar and Jack didn't want to become a drug dealer. Jack didn't want to see Manny leave, especially since he had no ideal of who would replace him.

Manny also had some "cred" as a tough guy. He never showed it but other inmates knew that he knew how to fight. Twice Manny stood up for Jack thus avoiding Jack's having the shit beaten out of him. Manny also advised Jack on how to behave and not offend other prisoners. Manny was a good cell mate.

Outside, in the prison rec area Jack sat in the dirt with his back against the fence. He watched the Black inmates lifting prodigious amounts of free weights. Black inmates controlled the prison by their numbers and willingness to do damage to other prisoners. The apparent leader was a guy in his mid twenties who could repeatedly bench press 240 pounds. He was 6' 3" tall and weighed 240 pounds. He lifted weights every day even in the hottest weather. Jack heard other men call him Steve.

Steve was a kick-boxer who practiced his art in the prison yard. Steve amazed Jack with his lightening speed. Steve was THE force to be reckoned with.

One day, when Steve finished his workout, he walked directly towards Jack. Jack looked around in hope that Steve was seeking out someone other than him. Unfortunately no one else was near Jack. He got ready to have the shit beaten out of him. As Steve approached Jack observed a four inch by eight inch tattoo on Steve's neck. The capital letters spelled "CRIPS". Jack was a dead man.

Jack was amazed when Steve extended his right hand. Jack shook hands while Steve pulled Jack to his feet.

"Black Steve," he introduced himself.

"White Jack," he retorted.

Steve laughed, "White Jack. I like that. Murder 2," was Steve's answer to the not yet asked question.

"Second degree burglary."

"I know. You were bad."

"It was my full time job."

"Who did you kill?" Jack asked as a joke.

"I was young. I would watch drug deals going down in a junkyard near my house in East LA. I'd sneak around to the dealer's car and show a 45. Everyone always surrendered the drugs and the cash. It was an easy gig until . . ."

"Until?"

"One dude surprised me and grabbed my 45. We fought but fighting in a car is tough. I had a spare leg piece, a 25 cal., that I fumbled for and finally pulled out. The guy was trying to get his hand on the trigger of the 45 so I put the 25 to his head and told him to drop the gun. He got ready to shoot me when I pumped two into his head. The guy still managed to get one off but he missed. I ended up putting four more into him. The guy just would-not-die. Cops came."

"The guy, of course, died. The prosecutor tried to get me on murder one but the jury handed down second degree. I was only seventeen."

"I heard about the million dollar jewel heist. You got balls."

"Thanks but that was not my biggest. I robbed houses for a long time. I really don't even like jewelry. Cash and gold. Gold and cash."

"Come meet my peeps."

Such behavior was unheard of. Steve introduced Jack to his rogue buddies and announced, "Hands off."

No one touched Jack.

Meals were always eaten at segregated tables. Sometimes both Jack and Steve would give the other food.

"Can't eat this Steve. It's bad for my ulcer."

"Here Jack. Chocolate pudding is bad for my complexion." and they'd laugh.

Sometimes Jack and Steve would sit together away from the others and plan strategy for future burglaries. In their hearts they both knew that they would never see each other after prison but strategizing passed the time. They were two men from vastly different worlds but they enjoyed each other's company. Jack, of course, very much enjoyed the protection that Steve's friendship offered. Steve had visions of being out on Jack's boat. Steve had never been on a boat.

"What's that tattoo on your neck Steve? Jack asked offhandedly.

"CRIPS. Its a gang. If you're going to survive today and you're bad and you're Black its necessary. Whites can't join. You white you know."

"I'm white. I know."

Jack was surprised by Steve's proper speech and grammar.

"Where did you learn how to speak so well? asked Jack.

"There was a teacher here who taught me how to read and she taught me how to speak. She was the kindest person that I have ever known."

"Ms Jackson?"

"Ms Jackson."

Both men would eventually be released. Jack would serve half his sentence and be released for good time. Steve served his whole fifteen year sentence. Steve's decision to serve the whole sentence was due to his not wanting to be on parole or probation. Both men would eventually be returned to prison through its revolving door.

BUTCH - CELL MATE #5

Butch was from Florida's west coast. He had been transferred from a federal penitentiary, where he served a five year sentence, to the Florida state prison to serve a second sentence. Butch was five years younger than Jack and outweighed Jack by forty pounds. Butch was in prison for dealing in oxycontin. Butch was a psychopath.

"We were big time, bragged Butch. We brought homeless people into Broward by bus, got them oxy scrips, filled the scrips, and then bussed them back after we payed them. We taught them what to say in order to get the oxys while they were on the bus. We even bought 'em lunch. We shipped them in from as far as Alabama. We did this once or twice a day. The oxys cost us fifty cents and we sold them for twenty-five bucks a piece. The scrips were usually for 100 pills. The buses held 50 people. We were pulling in a quarter of a million dollars a day. We couldn't buy and sell the shit fast enough. Feds caught up with us because of the huge number of scripts."

Butch showed no interest in Jack or anything that he had done. One day however Butch confronted Jack with a newspaper clipping about an sixty-four year old man that was accused of molesting a mentally disabled girl who was in the man's care.

"What's your name?" demanded Butch.

Jack looked at the newspaper article and showed Butch that the names were not even close. "Not only that, the guy is sixty-four. I'm thirty years younger."

The discrepancies didn't sooth Butch's rage. He was ready to show Jack some prison justice. Jack stood his ground and Butch finally backed down. It would have been bloody and both would have lost good time and possibly a body part. The incident was the scariest Jack had in prison - to that point.

ARIZONA - A NEW START

Jack was released from prison in 1986. The $200,000 that Jack had buried in his old back yard was gone, his homes were confiscated, his boats, cars, and aircraft. Even worse than loosing his possessions, Jack no longer had a driver's license. His girlfriend drove to Arizona where his modus operandi was unfamiliar to the authorities. Somehow, after his release from prison in Florida, Jack was able to beg and borrow enough money to buy a used Dodge Caravan. He sold the $7,500 Breightling watch for $750. The old van made it to Arizona without breaking down. His new girlfriend was talked into driving. She believed Jack's stories about Arizona being the land of milk and honey. Jack offered a freedom that his new girlfriend desperately wanted so she went along for the ride. The van became the couple's home and sole means of transportation.

    The good life was gone for Jack. Friends and relatives had long since severed relations with him. He had gone too far. Jack became a pariah.

    Jack yearned for the good old days when he had two homes, two boats, two airplanes, several cars and his beloved helicopter. He missed stalking and being able to outsmart the law and his victims. Even a great deal of his hair had found another location. Jack had no marketable skills to offer an employer. He no longer even had a strong back. Jack was a convicted felon.

In the previous seven and a half years his parents died, his sister had forsaken him, his girlfriends were gone, his agility was gone, and his youth had abandoned him. The only thing that he had left was his desire to get back to at least where he was before.

Arizona has homes similar to those in Florida and the homes occupants are similar in age. Arizona, unfortunately for Jack, does not have canals. Stalking a potential victim's home by car was hazardous but not as hazardous as breaking and entering a victim's home. People in wealthy neighborhoods don't park on the street. People in wealthy neighborhoods watch out for suspect vehicles. Residents of Arizona don't live in homes on the ocean front or Inland Waterway. Boat access wouldn't work in Arizona.

Jack considered using a rented car that would be similar to the victim's but having spent years in Florida prison left him without credit cards and driver's license. Without a credit card or license he could not rent a car. He would have to take the chance of using his own van.

Jack was broke when he arrived in Arizona having had all "his" assets taken for restitution. The twelve year old white Dodge Caravan would have to do. He did a fairly good job of lettering the old white van. "JACK OF ALL TRADES" was painted on the sides in red and blue. There wasn't even a fake telephone number. He painted it with paint and a brush that he shoplifted from a small hardware store. His girlfriend distracted the store's employees by screaming that an elderly customer had grabbed her so, for Jack, the paint, brushes, and masking tape were "free".

After several successful burglaries of lower end homes Jack felt the need to go upscale and get a bigger score. He didn't want to have to lug TVs only to end up with $25.00 for them. Security systems had been redesigned over the last seven and a half years and Jack didn't have the resources to update himself. Jack searched for houses that had old security systems that he was familiar with and hoped that the homes would also have older safes.

Jack's dumped the Florida girlfriend because she whined too much. He quickly found a new girlfriend who was less than half his age. She lived with her alcoholic, chain smoking parents in a trailer park. The trailer wasn't even a double wide. Jack and Sherry slept in the van in the trailer's driveway. Jack was bothered by his inability to control Sherry as he had done with every other of his girlfriend and wives. He didn't like Sherry's punk appearance and uneducated manner. Sherry was very willing to break the law if it at all appeared profitable. For now, she was the best that he could do.

Jack and his new girlfriend tried his previously proven technique of jewelry store shopping to find a mark. The couple's appearance no longer gave Jack the respectability that he had in Florida. The couple were asked to leave three upscale jewelry stores.

Jack's girlfriend drove around Scottsdale looking for potential marks when they were pulled over by the police for suspicious activity.

"What's the problem officer?" Jack yelled

over from the passenger's seat.

"License and registration," the officer addressed the driver, ignoring Jack.

Jack got out of the van and walked toward the cruiser.

"BACK IN THE VAN. BACK IN THE VAN NOW," screamed the cop who was standing along side the cruiser as a backup. He made a motion for his gun.

Jack realized that he was loosing his charm and cariama. His girlfriend looked like, and was, trailer trash.

The driver of the cruiser returned to the van's driver asking her to, "Please, step out of the vehicle."

"I wasn't doin' nothin',"

"Just shut up you dumb bitch," Jack thought.

Two backup cruisers arrived and the girlfriend was patted down by a woman cop and given a Breathalyzer. The resulting .06 wasn't an illegal .08 but it was a high reading for 10:00 AM.

One of the backup cops walked to Jack's

window. "Step out of the vehicle with your hands in the air. Spread your legs and put your hands on the roof."

"Am I under arrest?"

"No. Do you have any weapons on you?" questioned the cop as he placed his right foot to the inside of Jack's left foot in case he had to do a sweep.

"No. No weapons."

Jack knew that chatting with theses cops would not get him anywhere. Had his days of being able to charm police ended?

The cop patted Jack down. No weapons were found and a long look in the van's window revealed nothing suspicious.

The driver was issued a citation for not stopping for pedestrians at a crosswalk.

The girlfriend held the citation in the air shaking it angrily towards the policeman.

"What's this for?"

"Crosswalk violation."

"I friggin din'n not stop," She got confused by her own double negatives.

"Just drive," demanded Jack. The

girlfriend was less than half Jack's age. Her IQ likewise was half of Jack's.

Jack also didn't like that the girl was hard to control. Previously girlfriends who didn't listen to him could be badgered until they bent to his whims. The new girlfriend would end up badgering Jack until he could not take it anymore.

The couple was allowed to continue but the girlfriend was cited and Jack didn't like the attention.

Jack was depressed. He realized that when he had obvious wealth, the police were friendly and wanted to impress him. When one has a ratty old van and a ratty girlfriend the cops treat him like a criminal. "If they only knew."

Houses that he was relegated to breaking into had no security systems or safes but they didn't have any money either. He was averaging around $200.00 per robbery which was nothing like his scores from Florida. His difficulty was exacerbated by the number of dogs that the people had. He tried a taser and pepper spraying some of the dogs but got badly bitten by a German Shepard who just would-not-stop.

Jack finally found an upscale home on NW Street that fit his specifications.

Jack did his due diligence on the occupants and their house on the street with a lot of numbers, directional letters (NW) and even more numbers. Hometown, Reading, Massachusetts, had streets with real names and three digit or fewer house numbers. Jack longed for his Reading days

Jack was not happy with how things were going in Arizona. He would have to use his van, "JACK OF ALL TRADES", which he knew was only marginally evasive. Most neighborhoods just didn't feel right. He was familiar with the burglar alarm manufacturer of the house on NW Street. He knew that he had to make a big heist in order to get out of his girlfriend's parents' driveway. He also wanted to ditch Sherry.

Things weren't going well at all. Jack had to make the house on NW Street work.

Jack couldn't risk driving without a

license because that would be a parole violation and he really didn't want to go back to the can so, at least for the time being, Sherry would have to assist.

A BAD START

Sam came home unexpectedly while Jack was looking into the windows of Sam's house.

"What the hell are you doing?"

"Weeding," he answered as he reached for his fictitious work order.

Sam grabbed the work order. "What? You came from Florida to pulled my weeds?"

"No, I . . ."

"Get the hell off my property, bellowed Sam. Don't let me see you or this hand painted piece of shit van again."

The encounter was not a good way to start a relationship.

Sam reported the incident to Scottsdale police. Jack became a person of interest and his van's whereabouts was noted. Burglarizing the house on NW Street was no longer an option.

Jack got less and less cautious. He ceased to pre enter homes. Taking less time to stake out victims allowed more time for burglaries but cutting corners made him more vulnerable to getting nabbed. Jack tried again.

New Years Eve guaranteed that a young childless couple would not be at home. Jack pulled into the driveway on December thirty-first at 11:00 PM, as stealthily as he could. The home's security system was older so Jack was fairly sure that his tried-and-true method of disabling the system would work. Just in case, he would be fast in and fast out.

His attempt at disabling the home's security system wasn't successful so he tried a more barbaric method. Crowbar bar through the first floor bathroom window. Clear away the glass. Hop up and . . . Jack couldn't believe that he couldn't just hop up. He had gotten older and fatter. He was no longer a cat burglar. He used to be able to run and sprint out of harm's way. Jack's sprinting and hopping through windows days had past.

He pulled a chair from the pool area to enable his entrance. He glanced at the beautiful infinity pool which reminded him of the pool that his family had in Reading. The thought of his parents and sister saddened him. He wished that his life had taken a different course.

Moving the chair took precious seconds that he had not counted on. Jack continued on his mission not only to make a heist but also to prove to himself that he still had his youthful abilities.

Inside, he found the safe where it usually is in bigger homes - the hallway closet. The thought was, the burglars are going to find your safe eventually, so the owner might as well install it somewhere convenient for the homeowner.

The safe was shut but not locked thus saving precious time. Just when he thought that he had regained his lucky streak, his police radio blurted out a "62R" - residential burglary. Jack grabbed the cash, threw in in his bag and beat it out the front door. Before he could even get in the van he heard cars approaching and they were coming fast. Jack's hearing was still very good.

He dropped the bag of stolen merchandise in a neighbors bushes and ran to the back of the house. He heard the tires of high speed cars coming from a back street. Fences that he used to be able to hop over were now barriers to Jack.

The police found Jack hiding behind shrubs at the Scottsdale home. A canvas satchel with the home's cash was found twenty feet away from Jack. The police found a mere $305.00 and some broken watches in the canvas bag.

"No wonder the safe wasn't locked. It only contained pocket change," thought Jack.

As he emerged from the bushes with his hands in the air Jack looked past the gun that was pointed to his head and straight into the eyes one of the officer's, "It was the van right?"

The cop handcuffed Jack stating, "You should have just put JACK THE BURGLAR on the side."

Jack was charged with, and pleaded guilty

to, second degree burglary. Had Jack entered the residence a week later there would have been around $33,000.00 from rent collections. The owner of the property was a slum lord.

PRISON AGAIN - 08/13/91 to 01/23/2005

Jack was confined to prison on 05/08/1992 after receiving his second 15 year prison sentence. He was finally released on 01/23/2005. The time he served after his arrest on 08/13/1991 until sentencing in May of 1992 was subtracted from his prison time - "Time served". He was incarcerated in Arizona from 08/13/1991 until 01/23/2005.

Prison is a 7 X 10 hell on earth. Life remains in limbo in prison.

The pecking order in prison is determined largely by the nature of the inmate's crime. A burglar can have some status and Jack could con many inmates of the cell block by promising burglary work upon their release. Jack easily impressed some inmates with the vast sum of money that he had stolen in the past. Jack's bragging about the amount of goods he had stolen in Florida was simply not believable by some inmates. Some inmates thought that Jack's accounts were pure fiction.

Other inmates believed the rumors that Jack was a big time player but the amount that he had stolen was more than most of the other crooks could comprehend. For most of the inmates even one million dollars was simply unfathomable. Some of the inmates, however, did want "in" with Jack upon release. Jack played on the inmates greed. Jack knew that he would never trust any one of the other prisoners to partner up with.

Jack didn't have a Black Steve to protect him in Arizona. Jack tried to make friend with the tough guys but his age worked against him. He was too old to be a player.

While sitting in the "yard" Jack noticed a fat man with a salt and pepper beard talking with four very tough looking inmates. The fat man was a drug kingpin whose territory included Florida, Texas, Arizona, and part of Nevada. The fat man was a brutal enforcer and protector of his territory.

The men appeared to be looking at Jack and talking about him. Jack recognized the fat man's face but couldn't place him. Finally the fat man with his four man entourage walked over to Jack.

"Craig," stated the fat man.

"Jack," was the reply as he stood to shake Craig's hand.

Craig just stared and did not shake Jack's hand.

"You owe me three million dollars. Pay up."

The first blow to Jack's stomach knocked the wind out of him. By the time the four men had finished beating him Jack was a bloody mess. Craig just stood and smiled. Daily beatings would follow. Craig was a very bad man who had a great deal of power in the prison.

It was Craig's cocaine that Jack had taken in the duffel bag robbery at Windy Hill in Florida. Pay back would prove costly.

Jack was moved to a new cell block but that didn't stop the inmate assaults. The assaults were usually punches to his head or face. A punch to the back of his head might come from nowhere but the more threatening attacks came from guys who would walk up to him and punch him in the face. The face punchers were daring him to report the incidents. Jack knew better than to identify the attackers. A report of attack would initiate more vicious reprisals. Jack's situation was dire.

Jack wrote a letter of complaint to the prison warden. He finally got a meeting with a senior CO (Corrections Officer).

"We can move you to another block but nothing is going to change by simply moving you from block to block to block."

"Why don't you put the guys who have

assaulted me in solitary?"

"We don't have that many solitary cells. You will continue to be assaulted because of the nature of your crimes. I don't know what you did to warrant these attacks but get used to it. We can put you in solitary if you want but that will only mitigate the assaults."

Jack pulled his last defense, "I might just sue?"

"Get in line. Every guy in here thinks he's a jailhouse lawyer. What do you think you'll get, your own prison? You won't be out of here for another fourteen years. It's best not to piss off the prison officials and COs. By the way, worse things than getting an occasional punch in the face will happen to you. I'm surprised that you can still walk and pick your nose."

"I have some rights even in prison."

"You know, just because you've seen a couple of motions and figure that you can transpose dates and addresses doesn't make you a lawyer. Tell me, how do you spell subpoena?"

"I was never very good at spelling."

"Come on . . ."

"S-u-p-e-n-a."

"That's the worst that I ever heard it spelled. S-u-b-p-o-e-n-a. Some judges throw cases out of court when they see subpoena spelled incorrectly. Judges actually look for the misspelling."

"Just because I can't spell doesn't mean I'm not a genius you know."

"Jack, I have your records. Maybe you can convince the boys in here that you're a genius but I know that you are not a genius. You got caught and you were sentenced. You're not the smartest guy in the room. While we're at it, I've got your book here. You state in the book that you were a Mullins Baby Food baby.. Mellins Baby Food used to be made in Boston but there is no such thing as Mullins Baby Food. You were a Mellins - with an "E". "

Eventually, most of the other inmates stopped talking to Jack. When he tried to sit at a table to eat he was told that the seat he wanted was taken. And the next seat and the next. In prison one does not take another inmate's seat.

He tried to eat standing up but the COs yelled at him to sit down. He eventually had to eat in his cell. Finally all of his meals were eaten in his cell.

When he was in the main room he sat in a corner with his back against the wall but still other inmates landed punches or kicks. Jack offered no defense to the assaults. Jack would have repaid Craig but all he had left to his name was $28.35 in his prison account. Jack had fallen far from the days of helicopter flying.

Jack requested a transfer to another prison. The request was denied.

Jack, as a repeat offender, would not allow Jack to get get any "good time" off his sentence. He was sentenced to fifteen years and he would have to serve all fifteen years.

THE FUTURE - 2024 AD

Bob (RMHS65) bought Greystone at a foreclosure auction in 1991 - the same year that Jack was imprisoned in Arizona. Although, neglected for years, Greystone with its thick, grey stone walls and foundation, slate roof, and original amenities was well worth restoring. Bob did a fantastic job by adding gardens and refreshing the nobel structure, while keeping the original fixtures and features.

Bob made a few bucks in real estate which gave him the ability to purchase Greystone as a summer house. From 2001 on, Bob held a class reunion for RMHS65ers every summer. The reunions lasted a whole weekend. On Friday night, there is always a huge pot luck supper which was dubbed Italian Night out of respect of Bob's Italian heritage.

When Bob purchased the house vines grew inside through broken windows but the "bones" of the mansion were intact. Greystone's location in the Cape Neddick section of York, Maine is spectacular. The quarter mile long private road leads to a breathtaking view of the Atlantic Ocean and Nubble Lighthouse.

Greystone has four large living rooms, three kitchens, ten bedrooms, six bathrooms and a grand deck overlooking Maine's rocky coast.

There is a beach at the beginning of the access road. Gardens and lawns abound. Bob didn't restore Greystone, he brought the grey granite structure back to life.

The movie, "Bed and Breakfast", with Roger Moore was filmed at Greystone in 1992. The movie drags quite honestly, while Greystone itself steals the show.

The Greystone saga began: first Tyke, then Sally and others, all of whom had graduated from Reading High School in 1965 moved into the Greystone mansion after experiencing a series of unfortunate circumstances . Bob's wife drowned in a kayak accident less than 100 feet off the rocky coast of Greystone.

Bob found himself alone in the 20 room house devastated by his wife's death. Then Tyke's wife also died after her heart ceased to function. Due to the outrageous cost of trying to keep his wife alive Tyke found himself in debt and homeless a month after her death. Bob invited Tyke to stay at Greystone and Tyke gratefully accepted Bob's offer; "for maybe a month - I can always make more money," said Tyke

Financial constraints of Baby Boomers' retirement was exacerbated a year earlier because all social security benefits had been suspended by the US Congress. The Baby Boomers and their powerful voting block had been usurped by the Millennials' overpowering population in 2015. Social Security payments to retired Baby Boomers were financially breaking the Millennials, so, with their powerful voting block, the Millennials forced legislation that stopped all current and future social security payments and deductions. The Social Security System ceased to exist.

GREYSTONE GUESTS ARRIVE

Sally's husband died. Sally and Peter married right after college and bought a wonderful rambling New Englander home in Reading. Sally and the grey house were anchors for RMHS65ers. The couple raised two successful boys and became proud grandparents.

Many RMHS65ers went to Peter's (RMHS 1964) funeral and many tears were shed. Nobody didn't like Peter.

Sally couldn't decide where to live but knew that she couldn't stay in her house alone, knew that she didn't want to burden her children, and knew that she was far too vital for assisted living. Rich or poor, alternatives for older Americans simply were deficient so, as we always did, we took measures into our own hands and created a situation suitable to us.

"Sally, Tyke will pick you up in three days and bring you here to Greystone," Bob told her. Bob set Sally up with a Massachusetts real estate agent and trusted auctioneer relieving her worries and her children's worries.

Sally came to Greystone with only three suitcases. At seventy-five years old she was starting a new chapter in her life.

Sally was home at Greystone. There was no application, no financial disclosure, and no having to get to know new people whose trust had not been gained, and no confines to rob her of her freedom and dignity. Quite honestly, Sally had dreamed of living at Greystone since Bob purchased it.

Sharon was vacationing in Greece when she received Sally's email reporting her new address to her long list of former classmates and friends. Sharon immediately knew that she too wanted to live at Greystone and packed her bags.

Sharon email to Sally stated, "Sally I'll be arriving on Luftansa flight 7712 on Monday. Please arrange a limo to pick me up for a ride to Greystone".

Tom, the limo driver, arrived at Logan Airport Terminal E just before flight 7712's touchdown. The driver knew that he would have to wait for his customer to clear customs and pick up her luggage (the driver always called it luggage not baggage. Baggage is the thirty year old unemployed stepson who lives in your guest room and smokes pot all day).

Tom's attempt at phoning Sharon failed because Sharon had not activated her domestic phone coverage so Tom called Sally,

"Sally, can you describe Sharon for me so

that I can pick her out of the crowd? Her phone isn't activated domestically."

"She's tall and poised, has shoulder length light brown hair, and is seventy-five years old," Sally replied."

Tom imagined a wrinkled old bat. When he spied a very pretty tall woman with great posture and poise he thought, "That couldn't be the woman, she's only about thirty-five.

The woman made eye contact with Tom and smiled. As she approached he thought. "Maybe she's forty but that woman is no where close to seventy."

The woman opened the passenger's door and asked, "Tom?"

Tom told Sharon about how he had driven Colin Powell, Frank Sinatra, Bette Midler, and how Wade Boggs had given his nickname - all of which was true. Tom enjoyed the trip.

Everyone from Greystone greeted Sharon with big hugs and welcomed her "home". Sharon was in tears.

Then three others came to live there after the suspension of disability payments and

Section 8 subsidies by Congress. The Suspension of veteran's benefits by the US Congress brought in four more. Deaths of spouses and divorce brought in Sharon, Debbie, Wendy, Mary and Danny. Medical problems, divorce, death of partners and just plain loneliness brought more. The creeping years of the graduates of Reading High class of 1965 were good to some but not good to all.

Bob insisted, early on, that all Greystone Guests had to be graduates of RMHS65 - no exceptions. No spouses, children, grandchildren, great grandchildren, friends or other graduating years from RMHS were allowed. Bob realized that many RMHS65ers would eventually come as we aged, thus the restriction. And come we did.

AGING BABY BOOMERS

At our 50th reunion a few of the women still looked leave-your-wife-for-good good. Many others were still quite attractive. Some looked like Meatloaf (the singer not the food) but then, they looked like Meatloaf fifty years ago too.

In 2018, Cuba became a center for plastic surgery. Americans flocked to the island for basic face lifts that cost under $1,000.00. Face lifts could be gotten even cheaper in Venezuela.

In short, even an 70 year old women could look half her age or better. Because women looked younger they felt younger and they acted younger. Men, unfortunately, were in short supply. We still died earlier than women and men still went to prison at ten times the rate of women.

When we were born there were 105 males to every 100 females. By 2015, when we RMHS65ers were 67 - 69 years old, there were a mere 85 males for every 100 females. By 2025 there would be 2 women for every man. Ouch!

Since the ratio of women to men was so slanted towards men, most guys generally didn't opt for face lifts or other cosmetic enhancements. We aged and we looked like hell but the new improved women loved us anyway.

Men did have a secret weapon - we had Viagra3-105AA. Third generation Viagra with 105 milligrams for Advanced Age males. Unfortunately RMHS65 graduates all had 75 year old skeletal systems, 75 year old circulatory systems and 75 year old brains. We all had better lives but nothing was infallible or permanent. We were headed towards the end of our countdown.

One pleasant fall in the late morning Cindy, Sherry, Debbie and Sharon, after observing the sedentary male Greystone Guests and decided among themselves that something had to be done about the men's lifestyle. They were not complaining about our new (lack of) work ethic but were sincerely concerned about our health.

"They wake up around 9:00, read the newspapers and drink coffee, caffeinated coffee, until 11:00, and then have eggs and bacon for breakfast."

"Then they have a big lunch around 1:30 and have a couple of beers."

"Chores only occupy about two hours,

then cocktail "hour" begins."

"Then they watch sports programs until all hours of the night."

"Not only are they "belly big", I don't think that any of their arteries flow any more."

"If we say anything they'll go ballistic."

"OK. We'll get some very revealing yoga clothes today and tomorrow we'll surround them with encouraging attire."

"We could promise them all massages after the yoga classes. We can start with the Cobra and go to the Locust. They won't know what hit them."

"What the hell. No yoga - no massages right?"

The women's plan worked far better than they had anticipated. The guys were old but most of their plumbing worked and most of the women appreciated the lack of plumbing problems.

On the very first night after their first yoga class, the guys went to bed by 10:00pm. They slept soundly, awakening between 6:00 and 8:00. Oatmeal and fresh fruit were prepared and served by the women in their leotards.

"Yoga today?" Marty asked with a wide smile.

"Nope. Only Monday, Wednesday and Friday but we will stretch on Tuesday, Thursday and Saturday but there will only be massages on yoga days. Sunday will be an athletics free day and you can watch football all day," announced Sharon.

"This is June, so there's no football. Cam we watch the NASCAR race and Formula 1?"

"Yes sweetie you can watch bowling if you want."

"Works for me, Marty snickered. Works for me."

The guys got healthier, their plumbing worked even better, alcohol consumption decreased and the use of Viagra went down considerably.

Very late on a Wednesday night when all the others had gone to bed or were asleep in front of the TV, Sally and Tyke were in front of fireplace with fire almost out, facing each other on separate antique couches. Sally was enjoying

Jack Daniels on ice while Tyke had a Poland Springs. Tyke had been sober for thirteen years. Sally still enjoyed her evening "tea".

"What happened Tyke?"

Tyke didn't see that Sally had pointed to his leg that had been broken in a motorcycle accident in 1966. The leg had been in a cast for five years and had five operations, the leg had two holes (the result of osteomyelitis). The holes were big enough to insert fingers. The leg was a painful mess.

"Planet Earth continued to rotate and circle the sun."

"What?"

"We got old."

"No you ass," she giggled. "What happened with your motorcycle accident? The course of events."

"Holy shit. I never noticed it before. I should probably see a doctor."

A slight stream of tears trickled from Sally's eyes.

"You miss him badly don't you?" asked

Tyke.

"We were married for sixty-two years Tyke. Peter was the only man that I ever have ever loved."

"He was always fun to talk with. He was a genuinely nice guy".

Explanation of the motorcycle would have to wait for another day.

Two weeks later, in mid January, Sally and Lenny woke Tyke at 6:00 am. Eighteen inches of snow had fallen that night. It was still dark outside - Maine in the winter.

"Bob is having angina pains. He needs nitroglycerine pills."

"I assume that he's out."

"Out and the pharmacy can't deliver."

"Can't they send an automous4 car?"

"No. The pharmacist said that because of the long private driveway the automous delivery car can't read Google directions to Greystone." Lenny replied.

"I'll walk the three miles if we can't figure something out," Sally added.

Tyke looked out the bedroom window to assess the new fallen conditions.

"What do we have for vehicles?" Marty questioned.

Marty and Tyke shared a bedroom with bunk beds.

"We have Bob's Jaguar, your old Corvette Tyke, my '54 Ford and the house van." Lenny added.

"I'll take the house van. It'll make it. Front wheel drive with a heavy six in the front - that's all we need."

"Do you even have a license with an over 70 permit?" questioned Sally.

"Yep. Tyke stated proudly as he put on his pants."

The "boys" fired up the old van and headed out the unplowed driveway. Thankfully, the tires were good and the snow was powdery. There wasn't much gas in the tank but there was enough to go to the drugstore and then drive to the only place in town that still sold gasoline. By 2020, almost all cars used either compressed natural gas or were battery powered.

Tyke drove to the pharmacy. Lenny and Marty accompanied Tyke in case a push was needed but it wasn't. All three had driven in snow for over five decades. There was some slipping and sliding but Tyke kept the old van on the road. Experience still counts.

The van slowly ambled on the empty roads that led to the drug store. There were no car tracks to follow and strong gusts of wind blew the powdery snow in an effort to thwart the three occupants trek to help their friend.

"What's going to happen when Bob dies? asked Lenny.

"We will make it back to Greystone in time with the medication" Tyke emphatically stated.

"No. I mean when Bob dies. Probably he won't die today but Bob and Marty and you, I and all of us are all going to die."

"Its all in the group contract. We'll be alright. But for now, let's keep Bob alive."

Anyway, Bob got his pills, his angina was eased, and his heart got the oxygen it needed.

Greystone's nine bedrooms got filled up pretty fast. Soon the old friends were bunked two to a bedroom which was comfortable. We all protected Bob by not allowing anyone to even ask Bob to share his bedroom. Bob Eventually asked a couple of the guys if they wanted to move into his bedroom. Bob could hear the late night conversations and laughter from the other "dorm rooms" and wanted to be a part of that fraternization so Scotty moved a bed into Bob's room.

Within three years there were four to a bedroom. We referred to them as frats and sororities. They were all gender specific since the men and women loved each other but still wanted to scratch and prep separately.

THE DAILY GRIND

Many RMHS65ers were financially well off. Many were millionaires, some decimillionaires and two were centimillionaires. Money was not an issue. Food deliveries came daily. Everyone's blood pressure was taken on a daily basis and John made sure that everyone took their medications and yes we all took medicine for something.

Chores consisted of cooking, cleaning, gardening, lawn mowing, general house repairs (although no one was allowed on a ladder) and from 2:00 - 10:00. A revolving shift served cocktails. Everyone gardened. Politics was frequently discussed and occasionally the discussions got heated.

Newspapers were delivered every day. Good old fashion paper newspapers. We got three Wall Street Journals, two New York Times, two Boston Globes, the Phoenix Courier, the Palm Beach Post, the LA Times, and, of course, Reading's Daily Times Chronicle. A complementary copy of the Reading Chronicle was sent to each Greystone Guest every day. Yes, we recycled the newspapers.

Not everyone read the obituaries first (the so called Italian sports page). Coffee and newspaper reading was a daily ritual that all the guys and most of the women participated in before breakfast.

Almost every night someone would fall asleep in the den or in the hammock on the back deck.

A financial advisor used to come on a monthly basis but he was discharged because the residents were far sharper and more experienced than he was. Inexpensive general help did not seem to exist. In York and in most areas of the country, if a young person could do manual labor that person would start their own business and charge business rates. If repairs or improvements were necessary the Greystone Guests would do the work themselves. We had a great depth of knowledge.

Lenny and Peter ran the motor pool mostly which consisted of taking Greystone Guests to doctor's appointments and shopping.

Scotty and John kept the vehicles and the lawn tractor running.

Marty and Tom mowed the lawn.

Bob and Danny took care of finances, paid the bills and did legal work. Bob asked several times if we wanted a regular accounting of funds. Unanimously we decided that we did't need accountability. The decision never kicked us in the ass.

Sally, Susan, Dianne, Sharon, Wendy, Debbie, and Lydia cooked. Each prepared one meal a day every other day.

Debbie, Scotty, Mary and Cindy cleaned up after meals.

Everyone cleaned, inside or outside, for an hour every day.

Everyone, it seemed, like to tend the vegetable garden.

Most of the repairs were done by whoever was most capable. No one ever dodged their jobs or repair work. We were born to work and took pride in our endeavors.

Its been said that if one remembers the 1960s they weren't really there. We were having the 60s all over again. It wasn't too late for us to have a happy childhood.

JACK'S ARRIVAL AT GREYSTONE

Jack MacLean was finally released from prison and somehow made his way to Greystone. Around seven o'clock on a pleasant October night, George found Jack sitting on the front steps of. Jack had only a walker and the shirt on his back when he arrived.

George summoned Bob with an alert that brought everyone outside. Jack's appearance was shocking and not in a good way. His teeth were an absolute mess with his upper denture loose and cracked. His front teeth had been knocked out by fellow inmates so that he couldn't bite down when being forced to preform oral. Other teeth were missing due to decay and lack of oral hygiene. His once blond hair was mostly gone and the little left on the sides was grey/white.

The guy who used to run everywhere was dependent on a walker but he really needed a wheel chair. Jack had two strokes leaving his speech nearly unintelligible. He probably weighed 125 pounds. He was a mess.

Jack sat on step of Greystone's front entry way slumped waiting for our decision. None of us had any idea of how he even got to Greystone.

Having followed Jack's criminal escapades, the Greystone Guests were contemplating what to do with him.

"How did he ever get out of prison?" wondered Dianne.

"Some of the old timers are being let out so that the prison system doesn't have to deal with huge health care costs or body disposal," Kippy answered

"What do we do with him?" Questioned Susan.

"I don't think that he's a threat anymore but we can't take care of him. He's a black hole of need," Bob responded.

"We're not a nursing home," Replied Scotty.

"You're right, Scotty, but we owe him something. I still owe Jack $50.00 that I borrowed in 1966. Also, he used to pick me up and take me for rides after I broke my leg. And Scotty, you probably owe him something from when you used to "borrow" his MGA."

"I probably do. That was a fun car wasn't it?" Scotty recalled.

"It really was. We had some good times."

"Lets bring him inside. We can lay him to the couch in the den for the time being. We'll decide a course of action later," Bob decided.

It was Scotty and Ed who lifted Jack to his feet. Both guys had played football for Reading fifty-seven years earlier. Both were still tall and powerful. The two men walked on each side of Jack as his arms flailed around his supporter's necks. Jack looked like an old pair of pantyhose that had lost its elasticity

As Sally walked in front of the group, Scotty pinched Sally's still cute ass. She recoiled and yelped.

Scotty looked toward Jack with a "Jack did it" glance as he waived Jack's right arm in the air.

"You ass," declared Sally to Scotty as she walked to the rear of the clique. Sally smirked.

They brought Jack up the stairs and into the den. The guys gently placed Jack on the leather couch. Sharon put an absorbent pad under Jack. Franni got Jack a pillow and blanket. Liz brought water and Saltines..

Liz bravely gave Jack a sip of water through a straw.

"Thank you Liz," Jack managed and even cracked a smile.

The next morning a black coroner's van was at Greystone's front entry. The York police had been summoned and one cop declared, "We've got a cold one."

Sharon glided downstairs, in her Sharon way, only to be blocked at the den's doorway by the York police.

"Can't go in there."

"I want to check for algor mortis."

"You mean rigor mortis?"

"No algor - the decrease in body temperature."

"You a doctor?"

"No John is the doctor but he's asleep since he worked all night at the hospital. I'm a physical therapist. I did some postmortem work for the medical examiner in Burlington,

Vermont."

"Knock yourself out," the policeman remarked as he stood aside.

Sharon observed Dead Jack. He was still laying in the same position that he was in when Ed and Scotty brought him to the couch in the den the night before. There were no signs of trauma. His clothing was intact. The pad underneath him was wet from pee as she expected.

Sharon felt Jack's arm, chest, and toes. Since she didn't have an infrared thermometer so she guessed at Jack's body temperature.

She felt his neck muscles and then his arms. Rigor mortis had set into his neck and started in his arms.

There was evidence of livor mortis, pooling of blood in his back and butt.

"He's about thirty degrees Celsius, eighty or eighty-five degrees Fahrenheit. He's been dead about six or possibly seven hours. Don't put the time of death at midnight. Nobody can ever figure out the right date. Put either 23:59 hundred hours yesterday or 00:01 hundred hours today."

The cop was impressed. "What'd he die of?"

"Not sure. If I had to guess - ticker. Exacerbated by dehydration."

Pictures were taken, Dead Jack was placed on a gurney, sipped into a body bag, and wheeled away.

All of Greystone's Guests watched as the coroner's van drove away.

"Jack MUST be dead," Tyke told Sally.

"What do you mean?"

"Jack never ever let anyone else drive."

We didn't have a ceremony after Jack died, but rather a discussion. We really didn't talk all that much about Jack or his exploits, but rather we brought up all the criminal, sordid and unethical things that some of us had done. No one's admissions came close to the abundant evil that Jack had perpetrated but many of us had done some pretty stupid shit.

I was actually disappointed in our class to some degree. The most notorious student got his notoriety from being a thief. Not one of us ever appeared on Oprah or Letterman or held high political office. I had expected more.

After our discussion we had more discussions. That was a wonderful part of being a Greystone Guest - there was always someone awake and someone to talk to.

Some of us started to consider an "exit strategy". No one wanted to spend any time in the hospital and surely not an extended time. How much time did we have left? Who would be the last to go? What would happen when we were no longer able to run Greystone by ourselves? Finally, we figured that we would deal with THE END when the time came. We didn't dwell on our end game but there was one less of the 79 million Baby Boomers born in America.

We buried Jack in a respectable cemetery plot with an appropriate head stone. The stone's inscription read:

> John A. MacLean
> He was the best
> at

We wondered how well Jack would endure the heat.

JOHN ARTHUR MACLEAN   ARREST
RECORDS TIMELINE

NAME   FLORIDA STATE ID NO.
          SID NO.
MACLEAN, JOHN ARTHUR   FL-
01409675   1409675

FL ARREST 03/16/1979   AGENCY CASE
BS793227   OFFENSE DATE 03/16/1979
      POSSESSION OF STOLEN PROPERTY 03
COUNTS   STATUTE/ORD-FL812.014

      CHARGE 01 LEVEL FELONY ROBBERY
      DISP-CONVICTION CONFINE 15Y
CONCURRENT
      CHARGE 02 LEVEL FELONY BURGLARY
      DISP-CONVICTION CONFINE 15Y
CONCURRENT

FL ARREST 11/23/1981   AGENCY CASE 275398
     OFFENSE DATE 11/23/1981

          CHARGE 01   LEVEL-FELONY SEX
ASSAULT
          CHARGE 02   LEVEL-FELONY KIDNAPPING

AZ OFFENSE 08/13/1991 BURGLARY 2ND DEGREE
     ADMITTED TO AZ 05/08/1992 FELONY 15 YR
          RULING: NO CONCURRENT

AZ OFFENSE 06/01/1991 ATTEMPT TO COMMIT
SEX EXPLOITATION OF A MINOR
     ADMITTED TO AZ 06/15/1992 FELONY 16 YRS
          RULING: YES   CONCURRENT

FED RELEASED 05/13/1994   FEDERAL
REG#26938-008

FL ARREST 01/23/2005   AGENCY CASE
500501056
          PROBATION VIOLATION 001 COUNT
          STATUTE/ORD-FL948.06

          CHARGE 001 LEVEL-FELONY VIOLATION
OF PROBATION

FL ARREST 03/01/2005   STATUS RECORD NOT AN ARREST

FL ARREST 10/19/2012 WARRANT
    OFFENSE DATE 10/19/2012
    CHARGE 001 OUT OF COUNTY WARRANT LEVEL-FELONY STATUTE/ORD-FL901.04
    CHARGE 002 OUT OF COUNTY WARRANT LEVEL-FELONY STATUTE/ORD-FL901.04

FL ARREST 10/23/2012   AGENCY PALM BEACH COUNTY SHERIFF'S OFFICE
    CHARGE 001 LEVEL-FELONY, LIFE SEX ASSAULT - VICTIM 12 YOA OLDER
                STATUTE/ORD-FL794.011
    CHARGE 002 LEVEL-FELONY, LIFE SEX ASSAULT - W WEAPON OR FORCE SEX BATT

        VICTIM
                STATUTE/ORD-FL794.011

TERMS, DEFINITIONS, AND OTHER JAILHOUSE LAW

Laws, charges, and sentencing vary by state.

Breaking and entry: The criminal act of entering a

residence without authorization

B&E is a misdemeanor crime.

Possession of burglar's tools. Anything that can be used for forcible entry.

Is a Class A misdemeanor.

Robbery: Theft by force or threat of force. Robbery requires a taking of property from a victim, in the presence of a victim, or the proximity of the victim by the use of actual or constructive force.

First degree: Occurs when the victim is seriously injure or the perpetrator is armed with a weapon or what appears to be a weapon and threatens to use the weapon.

Class B felony.

Second degree: If there is an accomplice. If the victim is injured. If a deadly weapon is used.

Class E felony.

Third degree: Perpetrator uses force or a weapon.

Class D felony.

Burglary: Illegal entry with intent to commit a crime, especially theft.

First degree: Armed entry (what appears to be a

weapon is considered a weapon).   When the intruder causes physical injury. Intruder uses threats.
Class B felony.

Second degree burglary: Entering a building with immediate flight there from. Armed . Caused physical injury. Uses threats. Displays an apparent weapon. The building is a dwelling.
Class C felony.

Third degree burglary: Unlawfully enters a building with intent to commit a crime.
Class D felony.

Jail: Houses inmates who have been arrested and are pending a plea agreement, trial, or sentencing. Houses inmates convicted of misdemeanor crimes (typically less than a one year sentence). Houses inmates who are waiting transfer to another facility. Jails are generally run by county or city governments. There are about
3,600 jails in the United States. Broward County Florida maintains five jails with 4,800 beds.

Prison: Houses inmates who have committed felonies and have been sentenced to terms longer than one year.

Prisons are run by individual states or the Federal Bureau of Prisons.

Return the pen.

Made in the USA
Lexington, KY
27 August 2018